HOW TO SURVIVE YOUR FIRST YEAR IN TEACHING

Also available in the series

Teacher's Survival Guide: Angela Thody, Barbara Gray and Derek Bowden.

Getting the Buggers to Behave II: Sue Cowley

How to Survive Your First Year in Teaching

Sue Cowley

LONDON • NEW YORK

This book is dedicated to all the teachers, students
and loved ones who helped me succeed in,
survive and enjoy my first teaching job.

Continuum
The Tower Building
11 York Road
London, SE1 7NX
www.continuumbooks.com

370 Lexington Avenue
New York, NY
10017–6503

British Library Cataloguing-in-Publication Data
A catalogue record for this book is available from the British Library

ISBN: 0-8264-6465-3

Typeset by BookEns Ltd
Printed and bound by Biddles Ltd, Guildford & King's Lynn

Contents

Part II: You and Your Classroom

Part III: Climbing the Paper Mountain

Part VI: Onwards and Upwards

Acknowledgements

Special thanks go to all the staff who worked with me at Drayton Manor High School, especially John Rust-Andrews, Linda Huntley, John Browning, David Henderson, Simon Horne, Caroline Evernden, Luan Binnion, Jenny Burn, Chris Everall and Kate McClean. Thanks also to all my teachers at Kingston University and to Anthony Haynes and Alexandra Webster at my publishers, Continuum.

Extra special thanks and love go to my Mum, to Tilak, and to Álvie.

Introduction

So, you've worked long and hard to qualify as a teacher, after endless form filling and interviews you've found yourself a job, and now it's time to put it all into practice. But how ready do you actually feel to stand in front of a class and teach? And how do you deal with all the other aspects of a real teaching job? Somehow, that's something they forgot to tell you at college. Well, that's what this book is designed to show you.

When I started teaching I was amazed to find out just how inefficient schools can be: how much time is wasted on inessential, administrative tasks; how disciplined you have to be to spend your time in the most effective way; how stressful inadequate systems and ineffective management can make your daily life. I was also surprised to discover how a few simple but effective tips and strategies (some learnt from experienced teachers, others worked out by myself) could make such a difference to my success during that first, vital year.

In teaching, you are your own boss, and this is one of the joys of the profession. However, the job will expand to meet the amount of time you are willing to devote to it, and this means that you will have to develop self-discipline and time management skills if you are not going to be working until midnight every night. There are so many things about teaching that are learnt 'on the job', during that challenging first year or two. You will have to find ways to deal with problem students and awkward parents; decide how much time you can really afford to spend on marking; and develop a teaching style that works for all your children. This book will assist you in your quest to become the best teacher you can possibly be, by helping you deal with these issues, and many more.

I can remember feeling completely at sea at times during my first year of teaching, adrift without any certainties to anchor on to, drowning in a sea of paperwork. This book contains answers to all the questions I had and will give you guidance in overcoming the obstacles that stand in your way. This is *not* an academic textbook based on years of painstaking research. It is full of common-sense advice, based on my own experiences in schools, and all that I have learnt from other, inspirational teachers. I have combined practical tips and suggestions with examples (sometimes light-hearted) to help you succeed as you start out on your teaching career.

Although I work as a secondary school teacher, I actually trained to teach young children, and I am constantly surprised at how similar students of all different ages are. So many of the techniques that I used with 3-year-olds are applicable to 18-year-olds as well; so many of the challenges that face the primary school teacher are also the same as those encountered by teachers in the secondary sector and beyond So this book is aimed at *all* teachers, whatever age range you are teaching.

I'd like to wish you luck in your prospective profession – you have chosen one of the most varied, interesting and rewarding jobs it is possible to find. You have also chosen a career that is exhausting, often incredibly hard work and which may reduce you to tears from time to time. However, if you find that teaching is the job for you, you will be entering a worthwhile and rewarding career in which you will be able to make a real difference to your children. And with time and dedication you may become the most important type of teacher: a teacher that they will never forget.

Sue Cowley
www.suecowley.co.uk

Part I

Getting Started

Chapter 1

Survival tactics

Teaching can be a wonderful and fulfilling job, but there will be times during your first year when it feels more like a case of day-to-day survival. Let me start by assuring you that teaching really does get easier with time and experience. The learning curve during your first few years as a teacher is very steep indeed. In fact, each time you change school you will have to go through some of that learning process again, because of the different ways that schools are organized. However, once you are established within the profession, and have spent a year or so at your school, you will start to understand just why teaching is one of the best and most rewarding jobs that there is. This first chapter will help you survive that difficult early part of your career, and especially during your NQT year.

BEFORE YOU START

The weeks before you start your first teaching job are an exciting yet nerve-racking time. Your mind will probably be full of a combination of questions that you want answered, ideas about lessons you could do with your children and worries about issues such as managing behaviour and coping with stress. Here are a few quick tips to help you cope with the waiting period before your first teaching job starts:

- *Go easy on the planning*: Try not to succumb to the overwhelming temptation to spend the whole summer planning loads of wonderful and exciting schemes of work. Although you may believe that you are saving yourself time, you will probably discover that any detailed and in-depth planning done at this stage is fairly meaningless. Until you meet your students and get to know them a little, it is hard to anticipate their needs and interests. It is also likely that some (or all) of your teaching will be dictated by the schemes of work or textbooks already in use at your school. If you get the chance to visit your school before you start work, do ask about what planning it might be useful for you to do in advance.

- *Try to fit in a visit*: It can be extremely useful to visit your new school during the summer term. Although you will have been shown around on the day you were interviewed, it is worth taking another look when you are not feeling quite so tense. If you are not offered this opportunity, do contact the school and ask whether you might come in for a half or full day. You might spend some time looking at your classroom and deciding how you could rearrange the layout. You might also arrange to meet with some staff (see below) if this is possible.
- *Arrange a meeting with important people*: If the staff are amenable, during your visit it would be very useful to spend some time talking briefly to the people who will be important during your induction year. This might include your induction tutor, the current teacher of your year group in a primary school, or your head of department at secondary level.
- *Make the most of your holiday*: The best advice of all is to take a long and relaxing holiday before you plunge into the stressful world of the full-time teacher. Whether your finances will be up to this is another matter!

THE FIRST DAY

In reality you will have two 'first' days. Before the children return to school you are likely to have one or more INSET (In-service training) days; this will be followed by the actual start of term, when the students arrive back.

The INSET day

Your first INSET day may feel like an intimidating affair. The staff will probably be gathered in the staff room, chatting away to each other, discussing all the exciting things they did over the summer. You, of course, will know only a couple of people from your interview, probably the headteacher and perhaps the head of your department or your induction tutor. Here are some ideas and tips to help you get through the INSET day:

- *Don't dress too smartly*: It is highly unlikely that the staff will dress smartly on the training day. In most cases it is acceptable to dress casually, although if you feel uncomfortable doing this you could wear 'smart casual' clothing. The embarrassment of wearing a suit when everyone else is in jeans is something you could do without at this stage.
- *Be prepared for meetings*: It is likely that there will be a full staff meeting at some stage during the INSET day, in which the head will welcome everyone back, explain any promotions that have taken place and introduce the new teachers (including you). There may also be various administrative and whole-school issues to deal with, for instance, if your school is scheduled for an inspection. In the secondary school you may well have a departmental meeting and again there will be lots of administration to do – sorting books, checking deliveries and so on.
- *Use any preparation time wisely:* If you are allocated preparation or departmental time this gives you the perfect opportunity to become acquainted with the other members of your department or with teachers working near to your classroom. Do take care over the first impressions that you make: even if you are the most confident individual in the world, it is probably worth keeping fairly quiet at this stage to avoid making the wrong impression.
- *Start to collect resources*: The INSET day is the perfect time to collect the various papers and other resources you will need during your first week. These include:
  - a 'teacher's planner' (if your school uses them) – see Chapter 2
  - the finalized copy of your timetable
  - your class list or lists
  - details of any children in your class with special educational needs
  - copies of schemes of work and syllabuses (if possible)
  - sets of books or textbooks you will be teaching

- materials for artwork and displays
- exercise books and paper.

Do try to collect all the resources you may need now, so that you are fully prepared for when the students arrive. Exercise books and paper can be like gold dust at the start of term, especially if orders have not yet been delivered. If you are a secondary teacher with a form group, you will also need to collect diaries, timetables and other items for them.

- *Don't get too organized too soon*: When you receive a pile of papers on the INSET day, it is very tempting to start organizing them immediately: sticking your timetable and class lists into your planner, writing out your first week's lessons, and so on. It is best to avoid this temptation. The first week of school never runs quite according to the timetable – for instance, on the first day back the students may have assemblies and registration or tutor time. Class lists, too, are often subject to change when new children join the school or others do not turn up. Simply keep all your important papers in a folder to deal with at a later stage.

- *Spend some time on your room*: Some schools have problems with a lack of space, and teachers are forced to move around from classroom to classroom for their different lessons. However, if you are lucky you may be given a room of your own to work in and you could spend a little time before the students arrive stamping your personality on it – putting up a 'welcome' notice with your name on it and so on.

- *Get your bearings:* One of the greatest difficulties you will face at first is finding your way around the school buildings. If at all possible, spend some time walking around, preferably with someone who knows where everything is. It is useful to know the location of the following:
  - the school office
  - the student reception, if there is one
  - the head's office
  - the deputy head's office
  - the offices of senior staff, e.g. assistant headteachers, heads of year
  - photocopying machines
  - the assembly hall
  - the staff toilets!

The first lesson

So here it is at last, the moment you've been waiting for. Your stomach feels like lead, you're convinced you are going to be sick and your mouth is as dry as the Sahara Desert. Even the most experienced teachers find the first few lessons at the start of term difficult. How on earth are you supposed to deal with them?

Chapters 3 and 4 give you lots of hints on the management of behaviour and learning, but at this point I'd like to offer you a few tips and thoughts that might help you through this terrifying (and I'm not exaggerating) experience:

- *You are 'the mystery teacher'*: No one knows who you are yet. Your children may suspect that you are inexperienced, but unless you tell them, or give the impression of being scared, they have no way of knowing for sure. At the moment you are an unknown quantity and consequently you have an air of mystery that you can exploit. If a student asks you the question, 'Are you a new teacher, Miss/Sir?' simply answer, 'I'm new to this school.' At the same time, try to cultivate the sense that you have a wealth of experience behind you, teaching or otherwise. No matter how inexperienced *you* are, the students are always less experienced (and younger).
- *'They're more scared of you ...'*: You know the old saying about spiders and snakes: *'They're more scared of you than you are of them.'* Well, this saying also holds true for your children. All teachers have a window of opportunity in which to prove themselves to any class, a few lessons during which the students are still 'checking you out' and are unsure just how far they can push you. Think very carefully about your teaching style before you start. The old cliché that you might have heard at college actually contains a lot of truth: *'Start off by being as "hard" as possible, you can always relax, but you can never get a class back once you've lost them.'*

  You are not their friend, mother/father figure or counsellor, you are their teacher, and they will expect and indeed *want* a certain degree of formality from you. I'm not saying that you should scare the living daylights out of them, but do be as strict as you can. Once you become more experienced as a teacher, and indeed once you get to know your children during the year, you may well be able to relax. However, if you start 'soft', you are laying down trouble for yourself in the future. Honestly.

- *Set the boundaries now*: At this stage the name of the game is setting boundaries, letting the students know exactly what you expect of them (and why), what will happen to them if they do not follow your rules, and the rewards that they can expect if they do as you ask. Your boundaries should be fair, realistic and achievable. Talk to your class(es) about what you want and why you want it, and encourage them to respond to your ideas. This will help them feel more secure about how they should behave.

  The problem for you at this stage is deciding what your boundaries are going to be. Your school will probably have a set of classroom rules, but these may be rather vague. To a great extent setting boundaries is a matter of personal taste and opinion. It also depends a great deal on the type of students you have to teach. After a few years of teaching you will have made decisions about your own expectations but Chapter 3 gives some examples of boundaries, sanctions and rewards I would set for a class to help you at this point.

- *Wait for them*: In Chapter 3 I cover this idea in more detail, but it bears repeating a million times, and is never more important than on your first day with the students. Even the proverbial 'class from hell' will listen to you the first time they meet you. If you set the standard now, they will know what you expect. So, keep this in mind: *never, ever talk to a class until every single student is sitting still, in complete silence and looking directly at you.* The seconds while you are waiting can seem like hours at first, but set this pattern of behaviour now and I promise you that you won't regret it. Even if you find it difficult at first to utilize the rest of the ideas in this book, keep this one thought in mind when you start out on your teaching career.

- *Hands up!*: Start every question with the phrase, '*Put your hand up if you can tell me ...*'. This avoids the irritation of children calling out the answers and after a while you will have trained them to respond to every question by raising their hands.

- *Relax:* As difficult as it may sound, it is important for your own sake and for that of the children, not to rush your first lessons. Try to relax and never worry if there are pauses while you are considering what you want to do next. After a while it will come more easily.

- *Admin, admin, admin, names*: Bear in mind that there are a lot of administrative tasks to complete in the first few lessons that you spend with any class. Checking registers, explaining rules, giving out books and so on will take a great deal of time. Don't feel the need to rush into the curriculum. You need to learn the students' names as quickly as possible and you will also be finding out about their behaviour and how they work.

- *Use the register*: The primary school teacher, like the form tutor, must take the register to check that children are present at school. However, for the secondary school teacher, it is also worth getting into the habit of taking the register in every lesson you teach. When you come to write reports, you will need to know how good a student's level of attendance is at your classes. Taking the register will also tell you who owes homework and allow you to check for truancy. Above all, the register is an excellent method of control. If used at the beginning of the lesson it settles the class down, prepares them for the lesson, and you can mark as late anyone who arrives after the register has been done.

- *Who wants a job?*: Always, always ask this question when you have anything you want given out or collected in. You will find that your students are delighted to help you (especially the younger ones) and you will save yourself unnecessary work. You can even use the offer of a job as a reward if your class is keen. The same idea applies for collecting the register to bring to you at registration time.

- *Stand behind your chairs*: This may sound like a rather minor matter to be worried about when you have a million other difficulties to contend with. However, I promise you it is a worthwhile (and very simple) exercise which will help you control your class and also save you a great deal of time and effort. At the end of the lesson or the day, just before the bell or buzzer goes, ask your children to stand behind their chairs (or place the chairs on the desks) and wait for you to dismiss them. By doing this you have their attention in case you need to give out any instructions or reminders, you can walk around and check that there is no litter on the floor, and you have saved yourself the job of pushing in the chairs. Once you have set this pattern, you will find that the students stand behind their chairs automatically.

An extension of this idea is to turn the exercise into a 'game' for younger children. Tell them that they are being 'tested' on how quietly they can stand behind their chairs. This makes the end of the lesson nice and restful for you, as it avoids scraping chairs (and much quieter for the teacher of the class below you if you are on the first floor). A further extension is to then tell the children they must freeze as if they are statues until the buzzer goes. You could give rewards for this to encourage them, for instance allowing the 'best' children to leave first.

THE FIRST WEEK

By the end of the first week you will (hopefully) be finding your feet. If you are a primary teacher, you will be getting to know your children reasonably well by this stage. If you work at secondary level, you will probably have faced each of your classes at least once. You will also have an idea of what your timetable is like and the structure of your days. At this stage, there are a few things that you can do to prepare yourself for the weeks and months to come:

- *Get an overview*: At this stage it is helpful to gain an overview of the balance of your days and your week. It could be that mornings are a very intensive time in terms of your own teacher input, for instance, with literacy and numeracy lessons or with complicated A level classes to teach. At secondary level, there may be days when all the classes you face are difficult to control, and contain students with behavioural problems, but other days when you teach only well behaved Year 7s.
- *Plan for a balanced approach*: When you've gained an overview of your week, try and account for this variety in your planning. Do not plan whole days of lessons where you will be doing a lot of talking, as this will put a strain on your voice. If you do have to face a series of classes where the students are difficult to control, try to incorporate some lessons that will lessen the stress, for instance, visiting a computer room or watching a video.
- *Keep an eye on your marking load*: Some subjects, topics or lessons will create huge piles of marking, while others will give a relatively light marking load. Try to achieve a balance in your marking as well as in your planning. Keep an eye on the tasks that you are setting and ensure that you do not set too much work that requires detailed marking at any one time. Combine

oral, practical and creative work with written tasks, which are generally more time-consuming to assess.

DEVELOPING SUPPORT SYSTEMS

Whatever job you do, it is important to have someone to turn to for help: a shoulder to cry on when things are going wrong; someone to ask when you need advice or information; people to support you if others question your work. In teaching these support systems are absolutely vital. Teaching is a very difficult job and you will be put in situations where you are challenged in many different ways: physically, emotionally, psychologically and even legally.

So, start thinking about developing your own support systems as a teacher as soon as possible, preferably *before* you actually need to use them! Support systems for teachers come in a variety of forms; which one you turn to will depend on the type of problem you are experiencing. Here are some ideas about the different support systems available to you:

- *Your teaching colleagues*: You may find that there are surprisingly few opportunities for you to meet with other teachers, particularly if you are working in a large school. You will probably have contact with those who work in classrooms near to yours, and with other members of your department in the secondary school, but the majority of each day will be spent with your students. Although it can seem a lot of trouble for a quick cup of coffee, it really is worth trying to make time to visit the staff room on your breaks. Not only will you get the chance to chat to other teachers, but you will also give yourself a well deserved rest from the children.

  As soon as possible, preferably at the end of the first week, try to get involved in any social activities that are taking place (for instance, a game of football or netball, going out for a drink). One of the best resources in any school is its teachers and their experience. Once you get to know them a little, you can ask other members of staff for advice, for information, for a copy of that excellent scheme of work. You may also get a chance to moan or cry on a sympathetic shoulder. Your colleagues are a vital part of your support system: get to know them quickly.
- *Your induction tutor*: As a newly qualified teacher you will be

given an induction tutor – an experienced teacher who will guide you through your first year, watching you at work, assessing your progress, and checking to see whether you meet the induction standards. Your induction tutor should become a vital part of your support system, particularly if you find that you get on well with them. More information about induction can be found in Chapter 12.

- *Support staff*: A whole range of back-up staff play a vital part in supporting teachers. You might have the help of a classroom assistant, maybe you can call on the services of a science technician, or perhaps you have the assistance of a special needs teacher within your lessons. Make some time early on to sit down with your support staff to discuss how best you can work together, drawing on the experience and expertise of those people who work with and alongside you. Many of these staff will be able to offer you invaluable assistance in developing your own planning and teaching to suit your children.

- *Your head of department*: In the secondary school, the head of department (or faculty) is responsible for all the members of staff in a particular subject area (or areas). This person will have responsibility for what is taught and how it is delivered. He or she will also deal with any parent or student comments (good or bad) about your work. It is an excellent idea, both on a professional and a personal level, to develop a good relationship with your head of department. A good head of department will support you in times of need and will also help you to develop your career in the direction you want.

- *Non-teaching members of staff*: There are a lot of people working in any school who are not actually on the teaching staff: caretakers, receptionists, secretaries, accounts and office assistants, and so on. If you take the time to get to know them, you will find that they can help you out in many different ways. They will be able to make life much easier for you: smoothing your path when you want to arrange a trip; moving furniture for you at short notice; accessing computerized information; typing letters, and so on.

- *Teaching unions*: While there is no compulsion for teachers to join a union, there are many advantages in doing so, and a union can form a vital part of your support system. An important advantage of belonging to a union is the technical advice and support on legal and contractual issues that they offer. With all the stresses of starting work as a teacher, it is very helpful to gain straightforward advice on such matters. As a new member of staff you may feel uncomfortable approaching a more senior teacher with these questions: a union representative can offer you non-partisan advice. Most of the unions offer some type of discount for membership in the NQT year.

THE FIRST TERM: SEPTEMBER TO DECEMBER

Your first term at school will be a busy and exciting time. As you get to know the students and find your way around the buildings you will start to grow in confidence. Half-term will seem to arrive very quickly and your workload may even seem manageable This term is full of fun and excitement in the build-up to Christmas: there will probably be lots of events going on and you should really be able to enjoy yourself. There are, however, a few factors to be aware of at this stage:

- *Over-confidence*: Do be careful not to become over-confident and consequently relax with your classes too early. Your students may be responding well to the boundaries that you have set, but if you allow your standards to slip now they could quickly lapse into poor behaviour. It is tempting to let an air of over-excitement develop as the winter holiday arrives. However, do remember that you will have to face your children again after Christmas, when the end of the school year suddenly seems very far away and everyone gets tired and worn down.
- *Extra activities*: Beware of becoming involved with too many extra activities: the Christmas concert, the school play, working parties, the Parent-Teacher Association (PTA) and so on. It is very tempting when you start teaching to join in anything and everything to make a good impression. The other reason you may find yourself over-involved is that the older (more cynical, sensible or experienced) members of staff have developed the ability to refuse demands on their time. You, of course, will find it hard to refuse to take part if someone asks you to. Bear in mind that your teaching, and your children's learning, must always be your first priority.
- *Illness/exhaustion/stress*: You want to keep going, to prove to your

school that you are a reliable, hard-working employee. So, when you catch flu you muddle through and then you wonder why you can't shift the succession of colds that follow. Teachers are notorious for going to work when they should be at home in bed with a Lemsip. 'My classes need me,' they say, 'I'll only have twice as much work to do when I get back.' I know teachers who keep going and going and then every holiday, without fail, they fall ill.

A few points for you to think about on this one. Are you really so irreplaceable or important that the school cannot do without you for one or two days? Do you really want to pass on the flu to all the other teachers at your school? And isn't it better to take a day off now and then when you need it, rather than two weeks off when you finally realize that you just can't keep going any longer?

When you do need to take time off sick, make sure you follow your school policy on absence. This will probably involve telephoning the school to notify them that you will be away, the reason for your absence, and your likely return date. You may have to phone in for every day you are sick. You will also need to speak to the appropriate person to set work, and then 'sign in' on the day you return to school, registering your return with the school office.

- *Evaluation*: As an NQT your progress will be officially evaluated and some of your lessons will be appraised. Chapter 12 provides more information about the induction process. At this stage it is worth getting into the habit of self-evaluation, as this is one of the best, quickest and most readily available ways of improving your teaching.

If one of your lessons goes particularly well, take a few minutes to sit and think about what it was that made this lesson work, so that you can repeat your success in the future. Similarly, if a strategy that you adopt doesn't work, or if you find yourself in a confrontation with one of your students, think about why the problem occurred and how you might stop the same situation arising in the future.

THE SECOND TERM: JANUARY TO APRIL

Any teacher will tell you that the second term of the school year is the hardest. The days are dark and cold, with only limited hours of daylight (especially difficult if you teach physical education). The staff are tired and run down, and waves of illness spread through the school like wildfire, hitting both the teachers and the students. Spring and summer seem ages away and the rest of the school year stretches ahead of you like a prison sentence. You have the mother of all hangovers from Christmas and the New Year. The paperwork is starting to pile up and you're wondering whether you made the wrong career choice. Here are a few quick tips for getting through your second term as an NQT:

- *Plan a half-term holiday*: An excellent way of beating the second term blues can be to use the February half-term for a holiday. Don't take any work with you, escape somewhere relaxing and warm, and when your children receive an exotic postcard they will be impressed. If you do stay at home, you will no doubt end up working throughout your break, trying to deal with that pile of paper that has somehow appeared on your desk.
- *Reclaim your spare time*: If you did get involved in extra-curricular activities during the first term (for instance, the Christmas play or concert), you should find that you have some spare time on your hands right now. Of course you could use this spare time after school for work-related tasks, but it's worth considering whether you would be better off devoting some time to yourself, for instance, taking up some form of physical activity.
- *Experiment!*: As far as your lessons are concerned, now is a good time to take a few risks, to plan a few more unusual activities and see how well they work. By this stage, you will probably have developed a strong relationship with your children, and although I would still warn against relaxing with them too early, there should certainly be the opportunity to experiment a little in your lesson content and delivery.

THE THIRD TERM: MAY TO JULY

At last! The end of your first year is in sight. The third term always comes as a relief and is often a very enjoyable time. Examinations will probably be taking place, with some secondary students on study leave, hopefully giving you some extra free time. Although your marking load could become quite heavy, you will be amazed at how the word 'exam' turns your children into silent and hard-working young people. Here are some thoughts and tips for the summer term:

- *Enjoy it!*: Now is the time to relax and enjoy your teaching. By this stage your relationship with your children and your class(es) will be clear: you will know exactly who needs firm handling, and which situations or students allow you a bit more leeway. It is in the summer term that you can start to relax your strict teaching persona a little and get to enjoy your teaching and your children much more.
- *Use your time wisely*: It is rare in teaching to have any spare time, so think carefully about how best you can use it. It could be that for you, sitting and chatting with your friends in the staff room is the most positive use of a free hour. Alternatively, it might be that spending the hour doing some filing and sorting through your paperwork will give you a sense of real achievement.
- *Look for the best*: One of the key ingredients of a successful teacher is the ability to remain positive at all times – to see the best in every single child. A lot of schools have their sports day during the summer term, and it can be very enlightening to see some of your 'worst' or academically weakest students achieving excellent results on the sports field. Keep an eye open during the summer term for the different types of success that your children can achieve.
- *Beware of the weather*: A word of warning about the summer term: hot weather can create a sense of lethargy, both in you and in your students. I suppose it's up to you whether you decide to crack the whip, or (if you're allowed) to do all your lessons outdoors.

Chapter 2

Planning

Planning as a student and planning as a teacher are two very different things. The same applies to planning for an OFSTED inspection, and planning for your day-to-day teaching: the former is at least partly for show, while the latter is for your own classroom use. The difficulty during your first year is working out how to plan in a way that is effective for you. Planning, just like teaching and marking, is a very individual process. What works for one person may be completely unusable for another. In your first year you will probably find that you err on the side of caution, and plan in more detail than is strictly necessary. However, these detailed plans will not be wasted, as you should be able to reuse them in future years. This chapter gives you lots of ideas, hints and tips about how to plan so that you can start developing your own style, and find your own way towards really effective planning.

WHAT IS GOOD PLANNING?

First, let's take a look at what actually constitutes 'good' planning. Essentially, planning is only effective if it actually works for the individual teacher within his or her own classroom. The most vital component of a good plan must be that it leads to a high quality lesson, in which effective learning takes place. It could be that the children do not actually learn what was originally intended by the teacher in his or her plan, but that the learning outcomes are nevertheless very good. The tips below will give you some guidance in creating good plans:

- *Find a balance*: Above all else, you should aim to achieve a sense of balance in your planning. This balance is perhaps one of the hardest things for a teacher to find, and it can take a good couple of years before you feel you have got it right. This balance comes in two forms: there should be a balance within your working life between the time spent on planning and on other important parts of the job; there should also be a balance of activities within the lessons themselves. You can find much more information about balanced lesson planning in the section below.
- *Don't spend too much time on it*: If only it were as easy to follow this piece of advice as it is to say it! First of all, you will need to work out what constitutes too much time for you personally. Your first year will be busy, and your top priority should be what goes on in the classroom. Of course, your planning is all part of this, and you will obviously need to devote a fair amount of time to getting the lesson plans right. The secret is not to go overboard, planning in excessive or superfluous detail.
- *Make it work for you*: A plan is only useful if you can actually use it during the lesson. This is why too much detail can actually be a bad thing – if you find it impossible to refer to the plan quickly and easily, it will tend to stultify rather than aid your teaching. Alongside its ease of use, your plan should also give you sufficient detail to make you feel confident about teaching the lesson. If this means that you do wish to plan in great detail, then by all means go ahead, so long as it works for you.
- *Make it reusable*: At the opposite end of the scale from those teachers who plan in excessive detail are those who write down a few vague ideas minutes before entering the classroom. Once you are experienced, you may find that this is all the planning you require, but at this stage in your career you need to ensure that the plans are actually reusable at a later date. This means putting in enough detail so that you can remember the content of each lesson in the future.
- *Make it engaging*: To my mind, one of the most vital qualities of a good teacher is that he or she is able to engage the children in the work. A large part of this engagement is to do with planning appropriate, interesting, imaginative and creative tasks for your

students. Although we are constrained to a large extent by the demands of the curriculum, there is no reason why we should not strive to make our lessons as exciting and engaging as possible. You can find some ideas about how to do this later in the chapter ('Planning engaging lessons').

- *Make it work for your induction tutor*: Spend some time early on in the year talking through planning with your induction tutor. He or she will be able to advise you about how to plan, and also what is required during your observed and formally assessed lessons. It is likely that you will need to plan in some detail for assessed lessons, including information about special needs, differentiation, and so on.
- *Fit your plans to statutory requirements*: You may have wonderful and imaginative ideas for lessons that your students could do, but do check that they fit within the National Curriculum, or within the syllabus requirements at GCSE or AS/ A level.

BALANCED LESSON PLANNING

As we saw earlier in this chapter, balanced lesson planning is vital for a number of reasons, but in reality is hard to achieve. With practice, you will find that you can instinctively sense what is balanced and what is not. However, experience will only come by making mistakes in your lesson planning (and also by being willing to experiment with some more unusual ideas). Balance is essentially about lessons that utilize a variety of strategies, and which keep the students' (and the teacher's) interest. When you are trying to plan a balanced lesson, try putting yourself in your children's shoes and ask yourself how you would feel if presented with the lesson and activities you have in mind. For instance, how would you react if asked to read a difficult textbook in total silence for a full hour? Wouldn't you find it much easier if, for example, you had 10 minutes' reading time, and were then asked to discuss what you had discovered?

A balance of activities

It is not always possible to accomplish a balance of activities, for instance, if you are setting a test, but as far as you can, you should try to use a variety of different teaching strategies and learning activities in each lesson. By doing this, you will keep the students (and yourself) interested and engaged. You can also set a time limit for each task to ensure that the students work at their maximum capacity for as long as possible. A balanced lesson will not require the students to listen to the teacher for extended periods of time, or to work in silence for more than an optimum of about 20 to 30 minutes.

There are many possibilities for different teaching strategies and learning activities, and I would like to offer a few ideas and suggestions for you to try. Although traditionally associated with particular subjects, many of these ideas are actually applicable to a number of different areas of the curriculum. Be as experimental as you like – students respond well to the unexpected. I have also provided a model for a balanced lesson plan to show how you could use some of these strategies and activities within your classroom.

Teaching strategies

***Teacher based*:**
- Teacher talks to the class.
- Teacher gives instructions to the class.
- Teacher discusses a topic, getting responses from the class.
- Teacher asks the class questions.
- Teacher writes facts/figures/ideas on the board for the class to copy.
- Teacher writes the students' ideas on the board for the class to copy.

***Student based*:**
- Students follow instructions.
- Students work in pairs or groups.
- Students make group presentations to the class.
- Students make individual presentations to the class.
- Students brainstorm for ideas.
- Students work individually, e.g. reading, writing, drawing, calculating.

Types of learning activities

Reading activities:
- Individual reading.
- Shared reading, e.g. whole class.
- Reading for information.
- Memorizing facts, figures or vocabulary.
- Reading in pairs or groups.
- Speed or skim reading.
- Reading articles in newspapers.
- Reading from textbooks.
- Reading each other's work.

Writing activities:
- Writing essays.
- Answering questions, e.g. mathematical problems.
- Summarizing the main points of a text.
- Writing reports.
- Imaginative writing.
- Factual/analytical writing.

Drawing activities:
- Drawing diagrams.
- Drawing from life or photographs.
- Drawing from imagination or memory.
- Creating mind maps.
- Creating brainstorms.

Speaking and listening activities:
- Discussions.
- Explanations.
- Drama exercises.
- Role play and improvisations.
- Question and answer sessions.
- Quizzes (individual or group).
- Oral presentations.
- Debates.
- Making (taping) radio programmes on a topic.
- Listening to tapes.

Physical and practical activities:
- Games and warm-ups.
- Individual skills work.
- Group exercises.
- Drawing, modelling and painting.
- Practical experiments.
- Designing, building and testing.
- Performances/demonstrations, e.g. dance, drama, science.

A model balanced lesson plan

A balanced lesson plan of one hour could contain the following strategies and activities. I have assumed an actual teaching time of 50 minutes, giving five minutes at the start of the lesson for the students to settle and for the teacher to take the register, and five minutes at the end for clearing away. Although this lesson is for a writing-based subject, it could easily be adapted to fit a more practical area of the curriculum, for instance, science or PE.

5 mins	Introduction to the aim and topic of the lesson by the teacher.
	Teacher talks, students listen.
10 mins	Students brainstorm ideas on the topic in their exercise books.
	Students find out for themselves what they already know.
10 mins	Ideas are correlated on the blackboard and copied down.
	This brings everyone's ideas together.
20 mins	Students do individual writing on the topic.
	Focus on individual written work for a limited time.
5 mins	A couple of students read out their work.
	Brief oral presentation to the class.

Balance for the student

In addition to balancing the different strategies and activities used, the teacher should also be aware of what the students are being asked to do during a lesson. Is there too much emphasis on silent reading or writing, which requires a high level of concentration from them? Is there a great deal of noisy activity going on which may be disruptive for the quieter children (and other classes)? Again, put yourself in your students' shoes and think about how the lesson will actually feel for them.

Occasionally, your students will want to do very little during the lesson and you should be aware of when and why this might happen, and what you might do about it. There is little point in forcing your children to work in a particular way (e.g. writing in silence) if you are going to have to risk confrontation in order to do so, and if the work they produce is unlikely to be of any real value. For instance, a class that you see last lesson on a Friday, who have just had an hour of games on a really hot day, are highly unlikely to want to work particularly hard!

Balance for the teacher

While taking your students' needs into account, do not forget yourself. You should ensure that there is also a balance within the lesson for you – that you are not doing all the work or all the talking. When we first start teaching, our natural enthusiasm may encourage us to put huge amounts of energy into every lesson that we teach. It is only as the year passes, and your energy starts to run out, that you realize why it is so important to gain a balance for yourself within the lessons you plan. Here are some ideas about how you might do this:

- *Don't be excessively controlling*: As an NQT it can be very tempting to over-control your lessons, and to have far too much teacher input, using the 'chalk and talk' style above all else. The temptation is to lead from the front because this makes you feel more secure in managing your children's behaviour. However, don't be afraid to hand over the reins to your children. Often, the best learning will take place when the students are working in small groups or individually, with you standing back and simply acting as an advisor or facilitator.
- *Give yourself some time out*: You should aim for at least one period of quiet, calm individual work in each lesson if you can, preferably with the children working in complete silence. This will give you a rest from the noise created by a class of students. It will also free you up to go around and help any individuals who may need extra attention.

- *Take a lesson off*: From time to time, you may need a lesson off and there is no need to feel at all guilty about this. For some ideas about restful lessons have a look at 'Lessons for the tired teacher' in Chapter 4. Remember, although the students may feel that they work really hard at school, it is the teacher who actually makes the majority of the effort in most situations, including controlling a group of young people with a variety of different needs. So, when you need a break, give yourself one.

SHORT-TERM PLANNING

Short-term planning is daily and weekly, and perhaps also half-termly, planning. These are the plans that you refer to for each lesson, which give you an outline of what you are going to teach. As we saw earlier on in this chapter, for some teachers these short-term plans will be very detailed, while for others they will only act as a brief reminder of what is to be covered. The tips below will help you when working on your own short-term planning:

- *Balance your week*: As well as balancing each individual lesson, try also to balance your weekly lessons so that you are not planning too many teacher-intensive sessions in one day or on consecutive days. Bear in mind that you will be more tired towards the end of the week, and try to factor in some sort of restful work at this stage, particularly on Friday afternoons.
- *Balance your marking*: When you are looking at your overall plans for the week, try to set the marking you will do on a rota basis, so that you cover each class or subject adequately. Creating a rota will help ensure that all your marking does not come at one time. It will help if you identify specific pieces of work or topic areas (to yourself and to the students) that you are going to spend more time on marking. It can help to draw a brief overview of your week's lessons and look at how your marking load falls.
- *Be flexible*: During the day or week, you may find that a topic or lesson is going particularly well, and that it seems appropriate to spend more time on it than you had originally planned. Allowing yourself this flexibility is important, because it lets you respond to the mood and the reactions of your children. Never feel that a plan is set in stone and cannot be adapted as necessary.

LONG-TERM PLANNING

Long-term planning is essentially planning for an entire term or for the whole year. Your school or head of department may well ask you to set out in advance what you intend to cover, but do remember that they will not expect you to stick rigidly to a long-term plan. Long-term planning offers a way of balancing resources within a department or school. For instance, if only one set of books or other resources is available on a particular topic, efficient long-term planning helps ensure that they are available at the appropriate time. Here are some tips for long-term planning:

- *Be flexible*: Just as with short-term planning, flexibility is also crucial for the long-term plan. There are many variants in this type of planning, for instance, a topic may take far less time than you had anticipated, or you may find that the students are particularly enjoying an area of a subject and you would like to spend more time on it. If you are going to dwell for longer than anticipated on a particular topic area, check that this will not have an impact on other teachers who may be waiting for the resources your children are using.
- *Plan for variety*: Do try to plan the topics you have to cover in a way that gives the students some variety in their lessons. For instance, you could start by covering an area of your subject that necessitates a lot of individual work, and then follow this up with a group project. Similarly, a series of practical experiments or exercises could be followed by written review work.
- *Take an overview of the marking load*: Just as with short-term planning, you should try to take your marking load into consideration. You might plan to do some group discussion work just after a series of tests, or you could timetable in some practical activities at the end of a long written project. In this way you will not add to those piles of unmarked books or papers sitting on your desk, awaiting your attention.
- *Know your syllabus*: If you are a secondary school teacher delivering a course at GCSE or AS/A level, you will need to ensure that you cover all the areas within the syllabus. Bear in mind that it is better to finish early than to run out of time. If you have covered all the topics before the exams, then you can simply do revision work or perhaps redraft coursework.

PLANNING SHORT CUTS

During your training you will have been asked to give a large amount of detail in your planning. There are various reasons for this. When you first start teaching you are learning and experimenting and it is important for your tutors to see what you are doing and why. You will also have had a great deal more time when studying to spend on planning your lessons. Now, though, you have a full timetable and a large administrative workload. Should you continue to plan in such detail? As we've already seen in this chapter, the short answer to this question is 'no'. Above all you will need to find ways of keeping time spent on planning to a minimum, because you need this valuable time for other parts of the job. Here are some time-saving tips and ideas to help you:

- *Don't reinvent the wheel*: Teachers are notorious for redoing work which has already been done. If there are schemes of work in existence in your school or your department, and you could use them as they are or with minor adaptations, then why not do so? You could also ask other teachers in your school or department for advice on lessons that work well for them in each particular topic area, or with specific age groups.

- *Reuse your material*: If you are a secondary school teacher, delivering the same material to more than one class, why not use the same lessons with each one? A quick word of warning – do make sure that you don't become bored and stale with your lessons.

- *Use a computer*: If a basic outline format for planning is available, you will save a lot of time by simply filling in this outline on a computer. Many of the details will stay the same for a class from lesson to lesson (for instance, any SEN information or details of children who need differentiated work).

- *Use a project*: Although they are perhaps less fashionable than they used to be, I have had great success using projects with my students. One of the great things about projects is that they take up a number of lessons. I have also found that they do tend to offer highly motivational activities. Your lesson plan for a project might simply be a worksheet with a list of numbered tasks for the students to complete, and this is very quick to prepare.

PLANNING ENGAGING LESSONS

I feel very strongly that it is vital for us to engage our children in the work that we ask them to do. Not only is this important in creating a really valuable learning experience, but it is also crucial in maintaining good behaviour and in staving off boredom. Planning engaging lessons allows the teacher to apply some creativity, and to enjoy planning as an imaginative experience. There is perhaps a tendency to believe that older students will not react as well as their younger counterparts to unusual or creative lessons, but in my experience I have found that they welcome them with open arms. Here are some general tips and hints about how you can plan engaging work and lessons for your children:

- *Use props or objects*: Children do seem to find something captivating about seeing a prop or object in the classroom that would not normally be there. For instance, the teacher who uses a 'magic box' to inspire a lesson on story writing, or a selection of French foods to create some 'in the café' scenarios.
- *Use fictional settings and scenarios*: I have found that making the classroom appear to be somewhere different can be very engaging and inspiring for my children. I'm a drama teacher, though, and you may well be asking how fictional settings or scenarios could possibly apply to other areas of the curriculum. To give a couple of examples, the teacher delivering a lesson on bridges and spans might use a scenario in which the children work as engineers to find suitable materials to build a bridge across a shark-infested river. Alternatively, a teacher working on astronomy might ask the class to play the role of astronauts, and set up a space ship (using rows of chairs) which then flies out through the solar system and past the different planets.
- *Make it topical*: Lessons that are up to date, and which deal with issues of current interest to your children, will engage their interest and gain better motivation and behaviour. One example might be using the format of a popular television programme to deliver a lesson, for instance *The Weakest Link* or *Rikki Lake*.
- *Make it weird*: Teachers doing really strange things in the classroom will certainly catch the students' attention and make them keen to concentrate and learn. One highly original lesson I've heard of is the one in which a science teacher urinates into a bottle, distils the results and then drinks it! You might not feel

the urge to do anything quite that outrageous, but there are plenty of ways in which you can use weird and unusual ideas in planning and delivering your lessons.

THE TEACHER'S PLANNER

If your school uses them, the teacher's planner is a very useful way of keeping your important information in one place. The planner is basically a small (A5 size) or large (A4 size) book in which you can keep the type of information you would have kept in your teaching practice file during your training. The planner contains:

- a yearly calendar
- a page for each day's lesson planning
- space for registers
- a page to write out your timetable
- various other sections for notes, orders, etc.

Teachers use these planners in a variety of ways: some fill them out religiously in advance for each day, giving lots of detail about the lessons they will be teaching; others use them in a more haphazard style, filling them out after their lessons, perhaps as a reminder of what they have covered. It is useful to keep as much information as you possibly can in the planner, as it is then all in one place and you can carry it around easily. For instance, if you are a secondary teacher, rather than using a mark book you could keep all your registers, seating plans and marks for each class in the same section of the planner. In this way, after taking the register you can leave the planner open to refer to students' names, check who owes homework and so on. You could also write detentions in on the daily planning page, where you can cross them off when they have been served.

When you receive your planner, wait a short while before filling in registers, as there will often be changes to class lists at the beginning of term. Rather than writing this information out, it is easier and quicker to photocopy it to size and stick it in. Similarly, glue your school calendar in on the appropriate pages rather than spending valuable time writing it out. You will, of course, experiment to find your own way of using the planner. Do remember, though, that keeping all your information in the same place will make life much easier for you.

Part II

You and Your Classroom

Chapter 3

Behaviour management

For many NQTs, being able to manage their children's behaviour is probably the biggest concern that they have. In fact, managing behaviour is a worry for many experienced teachers as well. It is in our first year that we tend to make lots of mistakes, and I know I certainly did! However, if you can arm yourself with a good understanding of practical strategies for behaviour management before you enter the classroom, you will hopefully be able to have a more successful, and less stressful, induction year.

Depending on the type of school you are teaching at, classroom control may pose little problem, or it may be the most vital part of your job. However, even in the easiest of schools, where the students are keen to do whatever you ask, the importance of effective behaviour management should not be underestimated. In a school where the majority of students are well behaved, you may find that a relatively small number of students (perhaps those with behavioural special needs) create problems for you. In other schools, you could be faced with large numbers of children who simply will not do as you ask. By following the suggestions in this chapter, you should be able to make even the most difficult classes respond well. For more detailed and comprehensive advice, and lots of practical strategies to try out with your children, you could read my book *Getting the Buggers to Behave*.

WHAT YOU NEED TO KNOW

Before you even set foot in the classroom, there are a number of things that you need to know in order to be able to manage behaviour in the best way possible. Spend some time, preferably before term starts, finding out about and considering your approach to the following areas:

- *Your whole school behaviour policy*: If your school has specific policies it is best to stick to these, as the students will see you as a teacher who is aware of school rules and routines. It will be much harder for you if there is no school behaviour policy, but thankfully most schools now have at least some sort of whole-school policy in place. Many behaviour policies operate some kind of warnings system, whereby the children have a number of opportunities to comply with what the teacher requires before a sanction is given. For instance, you might be asked to apply a verbal, then a written warning, before giving a punishment.

- *What sanctions are available*: Your school behaviour policy should lay down clearly exactly what sanctions are available for you to use, and the circumstances in which you might apply them. It is vital that, before you face a class for the first time, you know the sanctions you are going to give for misbehaviour and also how serious you consider various types of misbehaviour to be. If you are as clear as possible about this, you can communicate your understanding to the class. On the other hand, if the students sense you are unsure about how to deal with them, they will 'try you out' and see how far they can push you. In the section below, you can find some general information about misdemeanours and their likely consequences.

- *What to do if sanctions are not served*: As well as finding out the sanctions for various types of misbehaviour, it is also essential that you find out what happens when a student fails to serve a detention or other type of punishment. If a student misses a detention and you do not follow it up, you may as well have given no punishment at all. You will find that this chasing up takes quite a lot of time at first, but once the students realize that they cannot get away with missing your detentions, your workload will start to lessen.

- *What rewards are available*: In addition to finding out about the sanctions that are available, do ensure that you discover what rewards you might use. Giving a reward is nearly always a more effective path to good behaviour than giving a punishment. If you can catch your children behaving well, and reward them for this, you will often find that misbehaving does not even occur to them. You will also create a much more positive atmosphere in your classroom.

- *What to do in a crisis*: Sadly, it is the case that in some schools there will be children whose behaviour can become so out of control that there is no way for the teacher to deal with it alone. Find out what you should do if a crisis situation arises, and who will be there to support you in resolving the problem. For instance, your school might run a 'red card' system, whereby you send a trusted child to the office with a red card, indicating that you need help immediately from a senior member of staff.
- *What your expectations are*: As well as discovering how the systems at your school work, you will also need to think about your own standards and expectations. If you can have a very clear idea about what you do and don't expect from your children before you ever meet them, this will help you in dealing with the management of behaviour. See 'Setting the boundaries' further on in this chapter for some more ideas about this.

SAMPLE BEHAVIOURS AND SANCTIONS

Below you can find some examples of misbehaviour, and some suggested sanctions for dealing with them. You may feel that some of these types of misbehaviour deserve stricter or softer punishments. It is really entirely a matter of personal taste and opinion. Choose your own sanction, or find out the school policy, for each of the following misdemeanours *before* you start to teach:

Low-level misdemeanours

For example:

- minor rudeness to other students
- forgetting equipment
- not doing homework
- talking repeatedly, and so on.

The punishment for this type of misbehaviour might be a detention of 10 or 15 minutes. It is best if this takes place with you supervising and on the same day as the misdemeanour occurs (i.e. during a break or after school). It is absolutely *vital* that you remember to enforce any detentions you set. If you don't turn up (or if the child fails to attend) the sanction is worthless and, in fact, this is probably worse than imposing no sanction at all. A useful tip is to write the student's name down, in your planner if you have one, and then cross it off when the detention has been served. Other sanctions that might be used for low-level disruptions include loss of privileges or points, letters home (for repeated offences), being removed from the classroom for a brief period of time, and so on.

Medium-level misdemeanours

For example:

- minor rudeness to the teacher
- swearing, but not *at* anyone
- chatting repeatedly and refusing to be quiet
- refusal to complete work, and so on.

A longer detention might be given for these types of misbehaviour, perhaps 30 minutes, sometimes called a 'departmental' or 'subject' detention in the secondary school. The problem with a detention of more than 20 minutes is that you must notify the parents or guardians that the child will be kept late at least a day in advance. You may find that your school has a specific way of doing this, perhaps through student diaries. A more senior member of staff may take this type of detention. Again, your school could apply other sanctions, such as those listed above, for these more problematic behaviours.

Serious misbehaviour

For example:

- fighting
- serious swearing (*at* you)
- throwing dangerous objects, e.g. chairs
- completely ignoring the teacher's instructions, and so on.

Some schools have a back-up policy whereby the teacher can send the student out of the room and to another member of staff if a very serious incident occurs. Please do not become one of those teachers who sends such difficult students outside the room to stand on their own for the rest of the lesson. You are still responsible for a student, even if they are standing outside the room, and if anything should happen to them you would be accountable.

Serious incidents like these are, thankfully, reasonably rare in most schools. They should be dealt with at a higher level, but it may well be up to you to ensure the information gets passed on. Often students who are struggling in mainstream education stay there because teachers do not *write down* details of the incidents that take place. This written evidence is essential as it will enable more senior staff to take further action. Try to write your account as soon as possible, preferably immediately after the lesson. You may feel shaken up by this type of incident and it can be useful to talk to an experienced member of staff about what happened and why.

THE FIRST LESSON

In your first lesson you should concentrate on stamping your personality and expectations on the class, and on setting up a climate for good behaviour. But how exactly do you do this? With experience, every teacher finds his or her own way, but I would like to offer some ideas for you to consider before your own first lesson:

- *Don't try to do too much*: Curriculum-wise, it is best not to plan anything too ambitious for your first lesson with any class. It is likely that you will spend much of the time on administrative tasks such as giving out books and on talking to the children about your expectations. If you feel you have to rush through these tasks to get onto the work you have planned to do, this will cause you stress and may make the children feel hurried.
- *Have a confident persona*: The irony about getting good behaviour is that if you come across as nervous, your children will tend to pick up on your uncertainty and may well respond by misbehaving. But of course it is only natural for an NQT to feel nervous in his or her first lesson. However, do try to hide your feelings and have a confident, certain persona. Being well prepared and having a good understanding of the whole-school behaviour policy will help you to achieve this.

- *Seat your students alphabetically*: They will moan at this one, but it is an excellent way of imposing yourself on a class right from the start. It is also a good way to learn the children's names and you can use this as your excuse. Once you have the class sitting in alphabetical order, ask for a volunteer to draw you a seating plan. You can also offer to reward the class by allowing the students to move to sit where they want if their behaviour merits it. However, beware of allowing them to move too soon.

  There are two ways of approaching this exercise: if there is space outside the classroom, ask the students to line up and allow them in one by one. This will take some time and you do run the risk of the students misbehaving inside or outside the classroom while they are waiting. An alternative, and probably the better option, is to draw a seating plan before the students arrive and ask them to follow it. This should avoid the stress of a chaotic start to your first lesson. It will also demonstrate that you are well organized and ready for the class right from the outset.

- *Explain your rules clearly*: The temptation to dive straight into your first 'real' lesson may be overwhelming, but I recommend that you spend some time (perhaps 10 to 15 minutes) discussing your ideas about classroom behaviour with your children. This way they will know that you mean business and that you have a clear idea of what your expectations are. These rules will give the children the set of boundaries that they need. This idea is covered in much more detail in the next section and in the model lesson in Chapter 4.

SETTING THE BOUNDARIES

No doubt your tutors at college told you about the 'honeymoon period', the time when the students will do whatever you ask, before they have 'sussed you out'. Have no illusions about this one, it is true. For the first few lessons (if you are lucky) the students will sit and listen to you, seemingly absorbing every word you are saying. Then, just when you think it is safe to relax, they will turn into the class from hell.

So, how can you avoid this situation? Other teachers may tell you to learn from experience, that in a few years' time you will find it easy to control your children. This, however, is not much use when you are starting out as a teacher. The last thing you want is to spend a whole year suffering before you get a chance to make a fresh start with a new set of students. And believe me, once you have 'lost' a class, it is extremely difficult to get them back.

What the children really need at the start of your time teaching them is for you to set the boundaries for them. If you do this effectively, and *stick to it,* you will make life much easier for yourself. Spend some time explaining your boundaries during the first lesson, and preferably make a list to go up on the classroom wall where you can easily refer to it. Your school may have a set of boundaries in the behaviour policy that you can use, and you will also learn with experience exactly what boundaries you want for your own students. The list in Table 3.1 gives some examples of the type of boundaries you might set, and how they could be enforced:

Table 3.1 *Boundaries for students*

Boundary	Reason/reward	Sanction
No one talks when I am.	We can get on with the lesson. It's rude - I listen to you.	2 warnings, then a detention.
You arrive on time to lessons.	Lateness is rude. Interruptions are frustrating.	A detention 2x amount late or 2x lates = a detention.
Use appropriate language.	It shows respect.	Immediate detention.
Always try your hardest.	I want you to succeed.	2 warnings, then a detention.
Do your homework (properly).	You will improve faster.	Detention to complete it.
Sometimes we work in silence.	We can all concentrate. 5 minute 'time-outs' to talk.	2 warnings, then a detention.
Show respect for others.	They will reciprocate.	2 warnings, then a detention.
Do not call out - hands up.	We can hear the answer.	Ignore those who call out.
Write as neatly as you can.	I can see to mark it.	Redo work neatly at home.
Bring the correct equipment.	We can get on with the lesson.	Instant detention. (This is harsh, but they won't forget again.)

TEN TRIED AND TESTED TEACHING TIPS

Teachers are constantly bombarded with information and advice, and it can all seem a bit overwhelming at times. Perhaps nowhere is this more true than with behaviour management, because it is such a complex and subtle skill for you to acquire, and there are a number of different approaches that you might take. At this point, then, I would like to offer ten practical and straightforward tips for you to refer to early on in the year, or at moments of crisis or despair when it all seems to be going wrong:

1. Wait for them.
2. Perfect the deadly stare.
3. Strike a balance.
4. Put yourself in their shoes.
5. Avoid confrontation (also known as 'you get what you deserve').
6. Praise one, encourage all.
7. Quiet teachers get quiet classes.
8. Explain, repeat, explain.
9. Always set a time limit.
10. Give one instruction at a time.

Wait for them

If there was only one piece of advice I could give teachers about behaviour management, it would be this: wait for them. If you follow this strategy from the very start, your children will know that it is the way you work. Do not open your mouth until you have *complete* silence, and I mean complete. Do not start talking until every single student is looking directly at you. Even if you have to stand with your arms folded for 5 minutes (or more), eventually they should come to you. But if you fight for them at the start, it will only get worse.

This idea is so useful and important that I am going to repeat it again. *Do not open your mouth until you have complete and total silence and every student is sitting still and looking at you.* Fold your arms, look impatient, check your watch, take out the novel you are in the middle of reading, do some knitting, gaze at the view out of the window, but on no account talk to a class of students who are not listening. This one action will stamp a considerable amount of authority on you for absolutely no effort.

It can seem scary at first, but I promise you if you wait the class will usually come to you, especially in your very first lesson. If you start to panic try using tips (2) and (6) – the deadly stare and praise one, encourage all. If you still cannot achieve silence, keep your mouth closed and go and stand right beside any student who is still talking. Invade their personal space and they should quickly become quiet. Alternatively, write on the board 'whole class detention' and start adding minutes to this until the class falls silent.

In some very difficult schools, such low-level strategies may not work, and you may have to resort to more unusual or extreme tactics. For some examples of other useful approaches, see my book *Getting the Buggers to Behave*. Above all, my advice would be to strive to achieve this silence right from the word go, and not to give up until you have managed it.

Perfect the deadly stare

As a teacher, you have access to many different forms of communication, both verbal and non-verbal. Perhaps the most effective of all the available ways of communicating your feelings is the 'deadly stare'. Perfect this and you will never have to ask for silence again. You will be able to walk into a classroom and stare your students into submission. There is no easy way of describing the deadly stare, but you will know when you have perfected it. The deadly stare says: '*I am the teacher, I am in charge, and if you do not close your mouth, stop talking and wait for my commands, you are likely to suffer in the most horrible way known to humankind. So, be sensible, be quiet and let's get on with the lesson.*' And all that without opening your mouth! The deadly stare might include all or some of the following elements:

- fixed stare at an individual who is not doing what you wish;
- raised eyebrow to show your surprise at a student's temerity;
- pursed mouth to show disapproval.

Strike a balance

Teaching is about balance in so many ways, but unfortunately this is one of the hardest things to actually achieve. You need to develop a sense of 'where the students are coming from'. By this I mean they will react well to a teacher who moulds his or her teaching style to suit the class and the students within it. With experience, you will use a very different attitude and style with a class of 15-year-olds and with one of 11-year-olds, or with the well motivated 5-year-olds in your class, and their less enthusiastic peers. You will only be storing up trouble for yourself if what you demand does not match the capabilities and expectations of the class and the children. Here are some tips about how you can learn to strike a balance:

- *Be willing to negotiate*: Although for most of the time you do need to give an aura of complete certainty, it is a good idea to know when negotiation could be the sensible approach. For instance, a secondary level bottom set in an examination year may well be disillusioned with school. If they feel they are not going to do particularly well in their exams, they will resent a teacher who tries to force them to work hard all the time. Far better to reason and negotiate with them. Try asking them to work solidly for 20 minutes, then allow a 5-minute break for a chat, making it clear that this is a reward which must be earned by good behaviour.

- *Respond to the 'mood' of the class*: It is sometimes the case that your class will arrive in a 'mood'. Often, this will be influenced by the weather or some other external factor. In the secondary school, it might be due to whether their previous lesson went well or badly. If you sense that your class is full of enthusiasm and in the mood for hard graft, then capitalize on this by getting through lots of work. If you feel that the class is over-excited, you might want to spend some time calming your children down. If your class seems down and in a foul mood, you will need to work hard to create a positive atmosphere.

- *Show that you're human*: Although I have advised that you start out in a firm manner with your children, and stick with this reasonably strict approach for quite some time, there will be occasions when you can allow just a hint that beneath it all you are actually a human being. This might involve laughing at yourself when you make a stupid mistake; it could mean giving your class a 10-minute break at the end of a particularly hard day.

Put yourself in their shoes

This tip is worth following whenever something or someone is frustrating you. That brilliant lesson you spent three hours planning is going wrong? Put yourself in your children's shoes and try to see it from their point of view. What would they say is wrong with it? Why exactly are they looking so bored? The students at the back of the class keep talking and passing love notes while you are trying to explain the finer points of quadratic equations? Put yourself in their shoes – you were young once, sometimes school can be just plain boring, no matter how good the teacher is. Developing this type of empathy will help you evaluate the work you set, and the way you teach, from a far more objective viewpoint.

Avoid confrontation (also known as 'you get what you deserve')

If someone is screaming at you, how does it make you feel? Now think about how children must feel if a teacher shouts at them. You wouldn't behave like this if you worked in an office, would you, so why do it to your students? If you do choose to become confrontational with your children, be aware that they may respond aggressively in return. In teaching, you get what you deserve, and if you do not show respect for your students, it is far more likely that confrontations will occur.

Confrontations can arise for many reasons in the classroom. You're human, and sometimes controlling 30 (or more) students can be exhausting. At times, a child will treat you in a totally unacceptable way, and the natural response is to give as good as you get. Do try, though, to keep yourself calm at all times. You will get far better results by reasoning with someone rather than confronting them. Here are some useful tips about staying calm, and avoiding confrontation:

- *Build a barrier*: The normal human reaction to an aggressive encounter is to become angry or upset. Many teachers are faced by confrontational behaviour on a regular basis, and we therefore need to find a way to take a more reasoned and professional approach. It is a good idea to build a metaphorical barrier between you and the confrontational child, so that any poor or abusive behaviour simply 'bounces off' your defenses.

The ideas below will help you in building your own personal protective barrier.

- *Don't take it personally*: It is all too tempting to feel that the abusive student is picking on you personally, and to give a very emotional response to this 'attack'. In fact the child is often simply responding to a situation that he or she finds it very hard to deal with (perhaps being told off, or being asked to work on a difficult task). Try to view the behaviour as separate from the child, and see it as a symptom of a deeper problem, rather than any personal reflection on you as a person or a teacher.
- *Choose sympathy over anger*: Any child who becomes confrontational with a teacher clearly has a problem of some sort. To help you stay calm, and to defuse a difficult situation, try to view the aggressive individual with sympathy rather than anger. This approach also helps take the wind out of the aggressive child's sails and to lessen the likelihood of further problems occurring.
- *Try to apply reason to the situation*: Using your calm and unruffled persona, talk to the child about what is going on. Encourage the student to discuss his or her behaviour and what has caused it. Talk to the child about what will happen if the behaviour continues, for instance, that you will have no option but to apply a sanction.

Praise one, encourage all

You were no doubt told at college that praise is a very effective teaching tool. However, generalized praise (although useful) has its limits. Next time you want a class to behave in a certain way, try singling out one individual who is already doing what you want. *'That's great, Sundip, it looks like you're ready to get on with the lesson, because you're sitting really quietly and waiting for me to take the register. Well done.'* This is far more effective than moaning at the class to be quiet. This is also a good back-up tip for getting silence when 'Wait for them' and 'The deadly stare' are not working. Do try this tip out – you may be pleasantly surprised at how quickly and easily it works.

Quiet teachers get quiet classes

On one teaching practice I worked with a class that had two

teachers, one for Monday to Wednesday and one for Thursday and Friday. They were both excellent teachers, but one spoke really quietly to the class and the other was much louder. The difference in the classroom noise levels amazed me – with the quiet teacher, the children had to listen far more carefully, and so the class was quieter as a whole. Of course, the big advantage of being a quiet teacher is the saving you will make on your voice. For many NQTs, a strained voice can be a real problem, leading to sore throats and time off work. The other advantage is that a quiet class is generally less stressful and your children will be calmer and less excitable. Here are some tips about how you can become a quiet teacher:

- *Learn to hear yourself*: Take a moment, when you are teaching, to listen to yourself. How loud are you? And just how loud do you really need to be? As well as hearing yourself in terms of volume, do consider the tone of your voice, and how relaxed you sound. This will transmit itself to the children, and have a direct effect on their work and behaviour.
- *Learn to turn the sound down*: As you listen to yourself, think of the image of turning the volume down on a stereo and try to do the same with your voice. Very often, we speak much more loudly than is actually necessary, especially when we are in close proximity to our students. Obviously, you need to be careful not to take this to extremes. I have encountered teachers who speak so quietly that no one can actually hear them!
- *Try not to talk too much*: When we first start teaching, it is very tempting to do a lot of talking at our classes. You tend to feel more in control when teaching from the front, but this will put a strain on your voice and in fact it can be less effective as a teaching strategy. You may also tend to raise the volume gradually as you talk, without even realizing this is happening.

Explain, repeat, explain

One of the biggest problems inexperienced teachers face is the frustration caused by misunderstandings in the classroom. You know the scenario from teaching practice: you spend five minutes explaining to the class what you want them to do, they start to work, then a few seconds later three hands go up – 'Miss/Sir, I don't understand ... what did you say I have to do?' It is actually surprisingly difficult to give clear and straightforward instructions that your children will understand, and this is one of many skills that you will have to acquire during your first year or so in the job.

Remember too that the children are being bombarded with new information, particularly at the start of term and especially those new to a school. This is where the strategy of 'explain, repeat, explain' comes in.

1. *Explain*: Tell the class what you want them to do.
2. *Repeat*: Choose a student (perhaps one who looks as if he or she is not listening) and ask the child to repeat what you just said. If he or she cannot, ask for someone who can to raise a hand. By hearing the students' interpretation, you may find out that they did not actually understand the instructions you gave.
3. *Explain*: Repeat the instructions again in your own words, clarifying any areas of uncertainty, and then ask: '*Is there anyone who's not sure what we're going to do?*'

This might sound patronizing, but it really does help clarify any misunderstandings and also encourages the children to listen carefully the first time. There may also be genuine misunderstandings taking place, perhaps because you are not experienced in giving clear instructions, or the students are not yet used to your way of working.

Always set a time limit

As I've mentioned before, your children *want* boundaries. They are still unsure of where they stand in the world and what is expected of them. Even as adults we crave the security of knowing what we are expected to do. Why then, do teachers set a task without letting their students know how long they have to complete it? Always let them know, whether it is 3 minutes, 20 minutes or 5 lessons. Think about how human beings work – we are always more efficient when we have a deadline, for instance, in an exam – and use this to your advantage in the classroom.

Once you have set your time limit and allowed the students to start working on the task, give them a constant reminder of how long they have left. Your time limit can be flexible, according to how quickly you think the students are progressing, or you could say to them, '*When you see that it's 10 past 10, I'd like you all to stop working and wait for the next instruction. I'm not going to remind you about the time, I'd like to see how well you can observe this time limit yourselves.'* When the deadline arrives, some of the more observant students will notice and stop working. As the noise levels drop, the others will (hopefully) begin to understand what is happening.

Give one instruction at a time

As we saw above ('Explain, repeat, explain'), it is actually surprisingly difficult to give clear and easily followed instructions, which will be understood by everyone. It can, of course, be very tempting to give your class a long list of instructions to follow, particularly if you are setting a complicated task, but it is actually very hard for children (and adults too) to take in a lot of information at once. It is far better to give one instruction at a time, stopping between each one to ensure that the students have understood what you want them to do. Again, this will avoid problems with misunderstandings and students continually asking what they have to do.

When you are giving instructions, you may find that the children are so eager to get started on the activity that they go to start work the minute you pause for breath. A very useful way of avoiding this is to state at the beginning: *'When I say "go" I want you to ...'.* If your children do jump up, ready to get started, you can simply stop them by asking, *'Did you hear me say "go" yet?'* They will quickly become trained in waiting for you to finish, and to say, *'Ready, steady, go!'*

LEARNING NAMES

Knowing your children's names is absolutely vital for good behaviour management. However, there is no over-estimating how difficult learning names can be. This is particularly true for secondary school teachers of subjects such as PE and music, who may have a large number of classes, some of which they only see for an hour a week. There are a variety of strategies that you could use in order to help you learn your students' names, and I would strongly recommend that you put them into use immediately you start with any class. One of the simplest strategies is to use the children's names as often as possible, whenever you address them.

Until you have a good idea of the children's names, it is very hard to control them effectively. A reprimand is always much more powerful if you can use the student's name; similarly praise is far better if you can personalize it. You will probably find it fairly easy to learn the names of the 'good' children, who always answer questions, and the 'bad' ones, who are always messing around. However, when it comes to writing reports, it can be extremely embarrassing if you cannot remember which student fits which name (or even which gender they are). Here are a few ideas that have worked for me.

Name games

If you teach or are a specialist in a subject such as Drama, you will probably know quite a few name games already, which involve the children moving around in an open space. Unfortunately, for the majority of subjects, the students will have to stay in their seats. Here are some adaptations of drama games that you can use in a static position:

- *The adjective game*: The students find an adjective to describe themselves, starting with the same letter as their name, e.g. 'My name is Sue and I am stupendous.'
- *Pass the name*: To start, the student says their own name, and then the name of the person they are passing to. Anyone who pauses or makes a mistake is out. 'Tim to Anna, Anna to Chirag, Chirag to Shami', and so on. Ask the students to pass to someone of the opposite sex, to make it harder and to avoid friends passing to friends all the time.
- *Pass the name (version 2)*: This is a combination of the two games above and requires the students to remember each other's adjectives: 'Terrible Tim to Anxious Anna, Anxious Anna to Careful Chirag, Careful Chirag to Silly Shami', and so on.

Use a seating plan

Seating plans are especially useful in the secondary school, where you will have a number of different classes, but they can also be very useful for the primary school teacher. Once you have your students settled in their places, ask one of them to draw you a seating plan which lists the names of each child and shows where he or she is sitting. Not only will getting a student to do this work save you time and effort, but the children will probably know each other's names better than you do. Refer to this seating plan (which you might keep on the wall or on the same page as your class register) as often as possible. Whenever you ask a question of a specific student, always use his or her name.

Make notes on your register

A quick note on your register can be a useful way of identifying easily recognizable students, or of telling two students with the same name apart. For instance if you have two 'Emmas' in your class, but one wears glasses, you can easily write this beside the name. A word of warning here: make your annotations subtle and polite, because sometimes your children will ask if they can call out the register. This happened to me once, and it was only half-way through that I realized I had written some rather cutting comments beside the names!

Memory systems

Memory systems can seem rather silly when you have never used them before, but believe me, they work. There are various books on the subject that you could study if you want to find out more – I would recommend the writer Tony Buzan as offering a good starting point. At the most basic level memory systems require you to make links in your mind. The links you are looking for are ones that are easily memorable. For some reason the human brain seems to work better if the connections are weird or unusual.

Probably the best way to explain this is to give a few examples. Say you have a student called Jane, who is very intelligent, but whose name you keep forgetting. Try thinking to yourself, 'Jane has a big brain.' I know it sounds stupid, but the fact that this rhymes will make it more memorable. To make the link visual as well, you could imagine Jane having an enormous head to contain her big brain. Similarly, if you had a student called Mona who was always complaining, you could remember 'moany Mona' and so on. Physical characteristics can also give you useful memory hooks.

The gentle art of bluff

For the secondary school teacher with a large number of students (perhaps seen only once a fortnight), sometimes it just proves impossible to remember so many names. The week of reports comes and you are panicking. You only have one more lesson with these students before you have to comment on them. What can you do? Here are a few strategies that I am not ashamed to say I have used, involving the 'gentle art of bluff':

- *Question and answer*: Ask a question using the name of a specific student and then look to see who answers.
- *State your name*: Set a group or individual task and ask the students to state their names before they start their presentation.
- *Off you go*: Ask the children to stand behind their chairs or get ready to leave by name order. When you call out the names of the children you do not know, look to see who moves.
- *Ask for help*: Ask a child you can trust to be discreet for the name that you cannot remember. They will be delighted that you have asked for their assistance.
- *Name your reward*: Give out merit marks (or whatever rewards your school uses) and as you write them into the student's diary, check the name on the front.

YOUR TEACHING STYLE

As you look around your school and hear the students talking about other members of staff, you will start to see how teachers each have their own individual style, especially when it comes to managing behaviour. Developing your style is entirely a matter of personal taste, and of course depends a great deal on the class you are teaching, but in my experience I have found that some approaches are far more effective than others. It is worth considering the impact of the following aspects of your style on your students when you are looking at how to control behaviour and maintain order in your class.

What you wear

Obviously the way you dress will vary according to your age range, the subject you teach and the type of school you work in. For instance, if you are a PE or drama teacher, you may well need to wear loose clothing so that you can demonstrate activities for the students. If your school has a strict uniform code for the children, it is likely that the head expects the teachers to dress smartly as well. As an inexperienced teacher, I would advise against wearing clothing that is too casual. If you dress smartly you will give your children the impression that you mean business. The class will be making judgements about you right from the first moment they meet you, and it is important that they view you as professional.

What you say

The phrases you use and the way you speak will all communicate a certain style to your children. Not only does this apply to the way that you set work, but it is also an important part of how you discipline the children and maintain order within your classroom. You will probably find that you talk to your students in a very different way to that in which you talk to your friends and other adults. We all adapt the way we speak according to the situations we are in and the impression we want to give, so be aware of this, particularly in your early lessons. The ideas listed below give an overview of how your speaking style should appear:

- clear-cut
- unambiguous
- simple
- calm
- consistent
- controlled.

How you maintain order

The way you create discipline (or fail to) will give out strong messages about your style as a teacher. The ideal situation is for the students to view you as firm but fair. You should apply exactly the same rules for every child, but do be aware that certain situations and individuals will call for careful handling. The following words summarize many of the key elements of an effective teaching style:

- calm
- confident

- assertive
- assured
- certain
- aware
- positive
- firm
- consistent
- structured.

How you set and mark work

Again, the way in which you set work, and mark the results, will have an impact on how the students view you and the way in which they behave for you. If your lessons are interesting, well structured and have clear aims, you will maintain your children's interest and keep them engaged in the learning. If you set lots of work that you ask the students to complete quickly, but fail to mark, they will feel that you are being unreasonable. On the other hand, if you never set homework and allow the children to work at their own pace, they may well like you, but whether they will respect you is another matter. The teacher's expectations about the work that will be done play a vital role in communicating his or her style, and in setting up a climate for good or bad behaviour.

What you do

Teachers should be careful to avoid saying one thing and doing another. If you expect your children to behave well, but you treat them without respect, you are storing up trouble for yourself. If you set the boundaries at the start and stick to them in a fair manner, the children will know exactly where they stand. It is important for you to have interests outside school as well. Your students want to feel that you are human and that you take an interest in wider issues, including the latest cultural developments. If you can comment on matters of interest to them, or even incorporate them into your lessons, they are far more likely to respond positively.

How you set up your classroom

If you are a primary teacher, or a lucky secondary teacher, you will have a space of your own, a classroom that you teach in all the time. Be aware that the students will make judgements about you by looking at your room, and consequently make decisions about how they are going to behave, probably at a subconscious level. This process will be taking place right from the very first moment they arrive at your class. There are a number of ways in which you can influence behaviour through the way you set up your room:

- *Personalizing the space*: Before the first lesson of the year, it is well worth spending a little time personalizing your classroom space. This will help stamp your mark on the room and show that you are in control. You might put up a sign with your name on it, or you could create some displays about the work that will be done at the beginning of term.
- *The layout of the room*: There is a temptation to maintain the status quo in the way classrooms are laid out, particularly when we are new to a school. There is no reason at all why you should not change the layout of your room to suit your own teaching needs. Perhaps you might want to turn the desks to face in an alternative direction, or create different learning zones in the primary classroom. Again, this will help show the children that this is your space, in which you maintain overall control.
- *Rows vs groups*: Setting out a classroom in rows gives a very different message to grouping the tables. This is, of course, a matter of personal opinion as well as being dictated by the type of room you have. See the following section for more comments on this.

MANAGING THE SPACE

As we saw above, the way you set up your classroom will send out strong messages about you and will also have an impact on the way that you teach. It is worth thinking carefully about how practical your classroom layout is before you start. At the lower end of the primary range, there can be quite a lot of flexibility about how different areas of your room are arranged. You might have a place for art, another for sand and water work, a carpet for stories and whole-class discussions, and some desks for written activities. If you do plan to make a lot of changes to a lower primary classroom, it is probably worth drawing some plans before you start reorganizing the furniture.

Higher up the primary school, and in the secondary school, there are two basic ways in which the classroom can be organized: with the desks either in rows or in groups. There is no reason why you should not start with the desks in rows and then change the layout later in the term. There is also no reason why you should not move furniture for specific lessons, but do bear in mind that there are administrative problems associated with this that you must deal with. If you are a secondary school teacher using someone else's classroom, you will make yourself extremely unpopular if you move the furniture, but do not return it to its previous position.

Desks in rows

- *Advantages*: All the students will be facing the front. This makes it easier to check that they are listening and also enables them all to see the board easily. You can give out and collect in resources and books along each row, to make life easier. The students will view you as a 'traditional' teacher (not necessarily an advantage, but this can be useful with a class where behaviour is causing difficulties).
- *Disadvantages*: It is hard to do any meaningful group or discussion work without substantial rearrangement of the furniture. There may be the temptation to ignore the ends of rows, where you cannot see the students so easily. You will only be able to give individual help to two students at a time. This style of layout does tend to encourage 'chalk and talk' teaching, i.e. the teacher standing at the front, talking to the class and writing notes on the board.

Desks in groups

- *Advantages*: Group work and discussions can take place easily. You can also talk to a whole group of students at one time. You are forced to move around the classroom more and consequently this layout encourages an interactive style of teaching.
- *Disadvantages*: The students may not be able to see the board so easily. It is harder to ensure that all students are looking at you and not talking if some of them have their backs to you. It might

be harder to give out resources. In a poorly behaved class, the children could interpret this layout as the sign of a relaxed teaching style.

CREATING GROUPS

For some activities you will need the students to work in groups, and creating these can be a challenge in itself. I would advise against planning group work when you are very new to your class or classes. Spend a little time on individual or pair work first, so that when you do attempt a group activity the students have a very clear idea about your expectations of their behaviour. In this way, you are less likely to encounter problems. Before starting on any group work, there are various factors for you to consider:

- *Moving the furniture*: If you have chosen to lay out your desks in rows, make sure that you allow sufficient time for moving the furniture and returning it to its former position. Rather than having a free-for-all, it is worth taking some time over this and asking one group of students at a time to rearrange their desks. You will also need to decide on the best layout of desks for the type of work you want to do.
- *Combinations*: Keep a careful eye on the combinations in each group. You will need to ensure that any troublemakers are kept separate, as they have a tendency to gravitate together. You will also need to ensure that there is a good mix in each group, with leaders as well as followers, although do be wary of putting too many strong personalities together.
- *Teacher vs student groupings*: Before you go ahead with any group work, decide whether you are going to create the groups yourself, or whether you are going to allow the students to do this. If you are only doing the occasional bit of group work, there is probably no harm in allowing them to decide for themselves. However, if group work plays an essential part in your subject (for instance, drama or PE at secondary level), you will need to set the groups yourself to ensure that the children work with a variety of others, rather than just with their friends. This will also help avoid the situation where one (unpopular) child is left out of the groupings.
- *A good mixture*: If this work is going to go on for a while, you

should spend some time working the groups out in advance, so that you get a good mix in each. An excellent way of creating 'instant' mixed groups is by numbering the students. For instance, if you want groups of 3 and you have 30 students in your class, ask them to count around the room up to 10. All the ones will then work together, all the twos, and so on. This works for groups of any size.

Chapter 4

Teaching and learning

Although other parts of the job such as managing behaviour and dealing with paperwork often get in the way, teaching and learning lie at the heart what we do as teachers. As with many aspects of the profession, it is once you take on your first real teaching job that you realize what a balancing act your own classroom practice really is. There is simply no way that you can be at your peak in terms of the content and delivery of lessons at all times, and you will need to make some difficult decisions in order to help you survive and succeed in the profession over the longer term.

This chapter gives you lots of hints about effective teaching and learning. You will learn a whole range of ideas and strategies, including: why aims are so important; how to set up the pattern of your lessons; and how you might use resources within your classroom to the best effect. In acknowledgement of the reality of a teacher's working life, I have also included a section that gives you ideas for how and what to teach when you are feeling exhausted.

EFFECTIVE TEACHING AND LEARNING

Offering our children effective teaching and learning should, above all else, be an imaginative and exciting experience, both for the teacher and for his or her students. Sadly, the creative energy that we might spend on planning and delivering wonderful lessons often gets dissipated under the myriad strains of the job. Working with a curriculum that has become tightly prescribed may also have a negative impact on our enjoyment of classroom teaching. The tips below should help you maintain and develop your own teaching and learning:

- *Stay enthused*: As students we have enough energy to spend time on planning and teaching high quality lessons. Although you may not be able to offer your children a constant diet of brilliant lessons, it is important not to lose your enthusiasm for the whole process of teaching. Although this does require more energy from you as a teacher, in my experience, the positive reaction that you will receive from your children breeds more energy and leads to a much more positive outlook on the job.
- *Create and deliver engaging lessons*: As we saw in Chapter 2 ('Planning engaging lessons'), getting your children engaged in the whole learning process is an absolutely vital skill for the teacher to learn. A lesson that engages your class will actually require less energy from you in terms of classroom control, because your students will be too busy working to misbehave. In addition, the positive response of children to a lesson in which they feel engaged and interested will fire your enthusiasm as a teacher.
- *Take a positive approach*: Children are surprisingly sensitive to the vibes given off by their teachers. If you come into the classroom in a good, positive mood, planning to deliver an interesting and engaging lesson, this will rub off on your students and you will get a better reaction from them. On the other hand, if you feel negative or even bored by the lesson content and delivery, this will be picked up by your class and could well lead to problematic behaviour.
- *Use a clear structure*: Children really do welcome structure – the teacher who gives a pattern to the lessons and the learning, as well as to the management of behaviour. A good way to offer your children a clear structure is to state your aims very clearly right from the start of the lesson (see below for more discussion about aims). Structure will also be apparent in the way that you open and close your lessons, for instance, asking your children to stand behind their seats before the bell goes.
- *Set targets*: As well as enjoying a sense of structure, our students also like to have a target to aim for, whether this involves their work or their behaviour. You might set targets for how well the

work should be completed; you might set targets that define how quickly an activity should be done. Your children will then have something concrete to aim for and to achieve.

- *Use plenty of rewards*: Rewards work hand in hand with targets – if the children can manage to achieve 'x', their reward will be to receive 'y'. This target setting/reward giving helps to create a sense of partnership between the teacher and the class. You are asking your children to work hard, and you are rewarding them when they achieve what you know they can.

THE IMPORTANCE OF AIMS

I can remember very clearly my lecturers at college going on and on about aims, but they never made any sense to me until I actually started teaching. There is a whole range of reasons why aims are so crucial. You can find some of these listed below:

- *Setting boundaries for the learning*: The importance of having aims goes back to the idea of the students needing boundaries: they need boundaries so that they know how you want them to behave and, similarly, they need boundaries so that they know what you want them to learn. By setting an aim for each lesson, the teacher is simply giving the students information about what they want the class to achieve during that period of time. At the end of your time together, the class can review their progress to see whether the aims have indeed been realised.
- *Giving a purpose to the work*: By explaining the aims of his or her lesson, the teacher demonstrates to the students the purpose of the work they are doing. If your children can see that the work you set has a clear and rational reason behind it, they are far more likely to approach it with a positive and hard working attitude. It is also probable that they will behave better.
- *Setting targets to aim for*: You should state your aim at the very beginning of each lesson: 'This is what we are going to aim to achieve today.' This will give the students a target to aim at, just as setting a time limit for any piece of work does. You should then keep referring back to your aim during the lesson to keep the students on task and on target.
- *Creating a sense of achievement*: At the end of the lesson, you can use the aim to summarize what the children have done, and how

well they have done it. You can discuss with them whether they have achieved what they set out to do at the start. If they have, then they know they have learnt something – and praise is in order.

- *Creating a structure*: As we have already seen, children really do welcome structure from their teachers, and the same applies to the aims of a lesson. Once again, though, put yourself in your students' shoes. If a teacher just launches into a subject, without ever explaining what is happening or where the lesson is going, they will feel 'at sea' and unsure about what you require of them or what you want them to learn. The intrinsic human tendency to place an order or structure on our experiences means that, without realizing it, they will piece together exactly what the aim is for themselves. However, it helps to avoid confusion, and it saves time and effort, if the teacher does this for his or her students instead.

A MODEL FIRST LESSON

At this point I would like to offer a model for a first lesson to give you something concrete to hang on to. This is not a model in the sense of a perfect lesson, but it gives a suggested structure for you to follow. The structure that is seen here shows how you can create a useful pattern to your lessons, both in behaviour management and in approaches to teaching and learning. Giving your children a sense that the lessons follow a familiar pattern each time helps them feel secure in the structures you offer them.

The model lesson below is intended as a guide and is based on a first-year (Year 7) secondary school class doing a subject where written work is used, for example, English or history. However, many of the points made and strategies adopted here will apply to students of different ages and in different subjects. As explained in Chapter 3, the majority of this first lesson with a class will be spent on explaining your rules and expectations. These are taught in exactly the same way as the subject content of a lesson would be delivered. You will see the teacher using many of the tips here that were given in the previous chapter on behaviour management.

The model is set out like a play script: I have included details of what the teacher does and says, a commentary that explains the reasons behind her comments and actions, and also some possible student reactions (and why the students might react in this way). I have assumed a lesson length of about one hour.

(*The students arrive in dribs and drabs as they have had trouble finding the classroom.*)

COMMENT: The teacher does not feel this slight lateness is a problem in the first lesson with Year 7s and does not make an issue of it. This may be different with a class of older students who should know their way around.

(*As they arrive the teacher directs them towards the seating plan she has made and put up on the wall. They are to sit in alphabetical order.*)

Teacher: (*to individuals and small groups of students*) Have a look at this seating plan I've made and see how quickly you can find your place. Well done, Ahmed, that was really quick, you obviously want to go to break on time.

COMMENT: The teacher has challenged them to make the seating plan seem like a competition rather than a control mechanism. She has then praised an individual student by name (she knows his name from the position he is sitting in) to encourage the others, and hinted at a potential reward.

Teacher: While you're waiting for everyone to arrive, you can chat quietly among yourselves.

COMMENT: The teacher knows that there is no chance or point in getting the class silent and then being constantly interrupted. Far better to make them feel you have been generous enough to 'allow' them to talk for a while.

(*After a few minutes the students have all arrived and are seated alphabetically. The teacher has a copy of the seating plan in her planner, alongside the register. She now folds her arms and waits for them to notice that she is ready to start. They gradually become silent.*)

Teacher: Right, before I start I'd like to make sure that *everyone* is sitting still and looking directly at me. (*She waits a moment.*) As you know from your timetables, my name is Miss Cowley and I'm going to be your teacher this year. You can see how to spell my name, because I've written it on the noticeboard over there. (*She indicates the board and the students look.*) Now, in today's lesson we are going to aim to get through lots of administrative tasks: checking names, discussing our rules, giving out books and so on.

COMMENT: The teacher has waited for the complete attention of all the students. She has informed the class what the aim for this lesson is and why. She will refer back to her aim later, to ensure that it remains explicit.

Teacher: The first thing I'd like to do is to take the register, so that I can check that everyone is here and learn how to pronounce your names. I'll also be able to check that you're sitting alphabetically, as on my seating plan. If I do pronounce your name incorrectly please let me know.

Student: (*nervously calling out*) Miss, miss, I didn't realize we had to sit where you said. I'm in the wrong place. (*Other students start to call out that they're in the wrong places too.*)

COMMENT: The teacher should have stated, 'Put your hands up if you think you're in the wrong place.' She has also given rather a lot of information at once and this may confuse them (see Chapter 3, p. 45, 'Give one instruction at a time').

Teacher: (*waits for silence with arms folded*) Please put your hand up if you think you might be sitting in the wrong place. (*Thankfully only four hands go up.*) Now, one at a time please go and check on the seating plan where you should be sitting. You first. (*They do so and swop themselves around.*) Now, let's get on with the register. Ahmed.

(*As the teacher calls out each name she looks up to see the student to check that she is pronouncing it correctly.*)

Teacher: Okay, well done. That's how I will start every lesson, by taking the register, so that I can find out who is here and also check if anybody arrives late. As you can see, I have a lot of names to learn and I'm going to need your help to do it over the next few weeks. You might be wondering why you're sitting in alphabetical order, well that's why, so that I can learn your names. Once I have learnt them, and if I'm sure you are behaving yourselves very well, I might allow you to move to sit next to your friends.

COMMENT: The teacher has started to develop the idea of a partnership – they will have to help her learn their names. She has also explained why they are sitting like this, to pre-empt the question that would no doubt have cropped up soon. She has also made it clear when and how she will allow them to move to sit somewhere else.

Teacher: The first thing I'd like to do today is to explain exactly what I expect of you in my lessons. That way you'll be clear about what you have to do and about what you shouldn't do. If you have any questions at any time, please raise your hands rather than calling out, so that I can hear what each of you has to say. I'm afraid that you will have to sit still and listen for a while, but I'll try to be as brief as I can.

COMMENT: The teacher is now going to explain her boundaries to the class and she has referred back to the aim of the lesson. She has reiterated the point about raising hands to ask questions and has also explained why this is necessary. She has warned them in advance that they are going to have to listen carefully for a while.

Teacher: The first and most important rule in my lessons is that nobody talks while somebody else is, particularly while I am. Can anybody tell me why this is so important?

Student: I can, Miss!

Teacher: (*Ignores the student who has called out and checks seating plan for the name of a student who has his/her hand up.*) Yasmin, you've remembered to put your hand up, well done. Can you tell me why this is so important?

Yasmin: So that we can hear what you are saying, Miss.

Teacher: That's right. Very good. It's very important that everyone can hear what I am saying. You will also need to listen to each other very carefully. Now, what do you think the punishment will be if you do talk while I am talking, Yasmin?

Yasmin: A detention, Miss?

Teacher: That's right, but to show how fair and reasonable I am I will give you two warnings first. After that, if you talk again I will give you a 15-minute, same day detention which I will take. If you still keep talking, the detention will go up to 30 minutes. If you find it impossible to stay quiet, I'm afraid I will have no alternative but to send you to ... (the head of department).

COMMENT: By ignoring the student who has called out, the teacher has made it clear by her behaviour that she does not want them to do this, without having to state it explicitly. After the student has answered correctly she has used praise and then repeated the rule, developing the answer a little (see Chapter 3, pp. 43, 44, 'Explain, repeat, explain'). She has then gone on to make the sanction for this misbehaviour clear. The sanctions stated will obviously depend on the individual teacher or school.

Teacher: Now, my second rule is that you all arrive on time to lessons, so that we can start work immediately. Put your hand up if you can tell me what you think you should do if another teacher keeps you behind, or if there is any other reason that you are late. Yes, Ben, what do you think?

Ben: We should get them to write a note in our diary, Miss?

Teacher: That's right again. Well done. And if you come to a lesson late without a very good reason, I'm afraid I will have to keep you behind after school to make up the time. Now let's talk about how we should approach our work. Does anyone have any ideas about this? Put your hands up if you do.

COMMENT: Although it appears that the rules are now being opened for discussion, it is fairly straightforward to elicit the responses you want or to mould the students' replies to suit you. The teacher will continue to go through all her boundaries in this way (see Chapter 3) until the class have understood. It may be useful to write them down on the board as you do so. This 'setting boundaries' may take about 10 to 20 minutes, but it is worthwhile.

Teacher: Now that we've gone through the behaviour I expect in my lessons, I'd like to give out the exercise books. When you get your book I want you to write the following information on the front cover as neatly as you can. (*She writes this information on the board for them to copy: the subject; her name; the student's name and class.*) When you've finished doing that, I'd like you to sit quietly and wait for the next instruction. Any questions? No? Okay, who would like to volunteer to give out some books? Danny has his hand up and is sitting quietly, so does Claire.

COMMENT: The teacher has given clear instructions to the students and ensured that they get this right by using the board. She has also told them what they should do when they have finished – the students will complete this task at different rates. She has chosen to 'reward' the two students who are following her instructions by asking them to give out the books.

(*They give the books out. While the students are filling in the front cover the teacher walks around and checks that they are doing it correctly.*)

Teacher: Now, before we start writing in our new books, I'd like to talk to you about how you should set out your work in them and how you should treat them. I'd like us to find about five rules to go in the very front. Can anyone put their hand up with an idea? Yes, Chirag?

Chirag: We should write as neatly as we can, Miss.

Teacher: Very good, Chirag. Jenny, can you tell me why you think this is important?

Jenny: So that you can read it, Miss?

Teacher: That's right. It's very important that I can read your work, so that I can mark it. Before we put that rule in, though, there's something that we're going to need at the top of the page. Who can suggest what it is?

COMMENT: The student has indeed offered one of the rules the teacher wants, but before they write down this particular rule she wants them to say that they should always put a title and date at the top of their work. This needs to come first, as they are going to need a title for their list of rules. She has asked a leading question to get the response she wants. She can then write the title and date on the board and the first rule which will be, 'Always put a title and the date on your work.' After this she can go back to Chirag's idea and any other rules she wants. It is worth putting rules about how to work at the front of an exercise book, so that they can be easily referred to if the students are not following them.

(*Once the rules have been 'negotiated' and written up on the board, the students copy them down while the teacher moves around the classroom and checks how they are doing. After a while, some finish their work and want to know what to do next.*)

COMMENT: The teacher did not let the class know what to do after they had finished. There are two options now: she could stop the whole class and let them know what the next task is, or she could let these few individuals talk for a few moments until the majority have finished.

(*After a few minutes it is clear that most of the students have finished.*)

Teacher: Okay, I think nearly all of you have finished now, so I'd like everyone to look this way so that I can explain what I want you to do next. Anyone who hasn't finished can then go back to copying the rules down. (*She waits until she has everyone's attention.*) Now, I'm going to set you an exercise so that I can see what you are good at and what you need help with. Put your hand up if you can remember the rule I told you about what we do when we are working individually. Yes, Rizwan.

Rizwan: We work quietly, Miss?

Teacher: That's very good. You work in complete silence so that we can all concentrate.

(*The teacher now goes through the task she wants the class to complete, writing a title and the date on the board and questioning them to make sure they have understood.*)

Teacher: Right, if you look at the clock you will see that we only have 15 minutes until the end of the lesson. I'm going to give you 10 minutes to complete this task, so that we have time to clear up at the end of the lesson. Are there any questions? No? Off you go then.

(*The students start to work, but one of them, Emily, starts to chat to her next door neighbour.*)

Teacher: Emily, do you have a question that you'd like to ask me?

COMMENT: Roughly translated as, 'I've checked whether the class had any questions and they didn't, I've told you we're not going to talk while working, so why on earth have you started chatting?' Combined with the 'deadly stare' this will hopefully persuade Emily to be quiet.

(*Emily becomes quiet, but a few minutes later she starts to talk again.*)

Teacher: Emily, I have made it perfectly clear that you are not to talk while you are working, so I am now giving you your first warning. Do you understand?

Emily: Yes, Miss.

(*Emily becomes quiet again, but a few minutes later she starts chatting again to her friend, Jessica, who talks back to her.*)

Teacher: Jessica, I can see that you've decided to talk as well, so I'm going to give you your first warning. Can you tell me what will happen after your second warning?

Jessica: A detention, Miss?

Teacher: That's right. And it would be a real shame to get a detention in your very first lesson with me, wouldn't it? Now can you get on with your work in silence please and stop disturbing the class. We have five minutes left, everybody.

COMMENT: It is sometimes better to pick on the person who is being chatted to, rather than the one who is talking. This works because there is no point in someone talking if they are getting no response. The teacher has used this strategy and has made the sanction for ignoring her instructions very clear. It would be a shame to have to give out detentions in the very first lesson, but as it is almost time to finish, she will probably not have to do this. She has reminded the class about how much time they have left and will do so again as the time runs out.

(*A few minutes later.*)

Teacher: You have one minute left now, so I'd like you to try and finish off the section that you are doing. When you have finished, please close your book and make a pile in the centre of your tables. (*A minute later.*) Okay, time's up, please stop and put your books in the middle of the table. Can I have two volunteers to collect the books in please? (*Lots of hands go up and the teacher chooses two students.*)

(*When the books have been collected in, the teacher stands with her arms folded and waits for silence. She has overrun a little and the buzzer for break goes, but she does not move. Eventually the students become silent, the more observant ones 'shushing' the others.*)

COMMENT: It is really important to have an orderly end to the lesson, as it ensures the students go away in a calm frame of mind. They will hopefully remember your excellent classroom control for the next lesson. The teacher is fortunate that it is break next, as the students are keen to go out to play. If it was not, she would have problems because she would be making them late for their next lesson. It is much better to end too early, rather than too late. You can always 'string out' the standing behind chairs exercise (see Chapter 1) by allowing one group at a time to push their chairs in and then 'practise' standing in silence.

Teacher: Right, as you can hear, the buzzer for break has gone, but I have a couple of things to say to you before we go, so can I have everyone looking at me? (*She waits a moment.*) Now, first of all I'd like to say that you've behaved yourselves well this lesson and we've got through all those administrative tasks that I wanted to complete – well done. However, next time I see you I want you to sit in alphabetical order again so that I can carry on learning your names. Secondly, at the end of every lesson with me I will ask you to stand behind your chairs. When everyone is standing still and silent behind their chairs I will dismiss you one group at a time. (*Some of the students go to stand behind their chairs.*) I don't believe I heard anyone say, 'Stand behind your chairs,' did I? Please sit back down. (*She waits for them to do so.*) Okay, please stand quietly behind your chairs.

(*When they are all standing silent and ready she dismisses them, one group at a time, choosing the best behaved and quietest group first.*)

COMMENT: The teacher has praised the class to reinforce the behaviour they have learned. She has also restated the aim of the lesson so that the students understand what they have achieved. It may seem petty to make them sit back down, but it shows the class that they must wait for the teacher's command. By dismissing the best behaved group first, she is making a point about who will receive the rewards in her lessons.

LESSONS FOR THE TIRED TEACHER

In your first term of teaching, you will probably be full of enthusiasm and energy, rising happily to the challenge of any problems that crop up. However, towards the end of this term (or possibly half-term) you may well find yourself becoming tired, both physically and emotionally. Later in this chapter you will find more details about taking care of yourself and avoiding tiredness, but at this point I would like to offer a few suggestions for lessons you can use to add some variety to your teaching and give yourself a bit of a rest at the same time. Although these are obviously not lessons that you would use every day of the week, there is absolutely no need to feel guilty when you do need a bit of a break.

The important idea to grasp hold of is that it is the students who should be doing the work, rather than you. Individual exercises tend to be less teacher-intensive than group work, where you will have the problem of noise levels to contend with (a lot of noise can be tiring in itself). However, this is not always the case, for instance, in the 'Show and tell' activity described below. These suggestions are not subject specific and you should be able to adapt them to your own area of specialization or to your own age range.

Look it up!

Give each child a dictionary or a textbook. Make this a competition to encourage an enthusiastic response. The children must look up the word or subject reference that you give them as quickly as they can. When they find the relevant page, they should raise a hand. The 'winner' then reads out the meaning or passage to the rest of the class. If you have the energy, you can reward the children. One useful reward is for the winner to be given the chance to choose the next word to look up (this limits your involvement to practically nil!). You can also extend this exercise by asking the children to write down the definitions or passages into their exercise books. This will make the task a longer one and give you more of a rest.

Time for a test

Tests are always a good back-up for when you are exhausted, because they involve no teacher input beyond actually setting the test in the first place (and marking it afterwards). The class will have to work in silence, preferably for a whole lesson. The only drawback with tests is the marking involved. Adopt one of the strategies described in Chapter 7 to save yourself time.

Time for the television

I would guard against the temptation to show endless videos or television programmes to your classes, but there are certainly occasions when it is educationally justified and it is definitely a good way of having a 'lesson off'. If you are lucky, you may find a long video that takes more than one lesson to show. Ensure that the video links with the work you have been doing and make sure you book the equipment in advance. There is nothing worse than planning a television lesson and then finding out that the television and video are already in use. If you can, it is worth setting up the equipment before your students arrive, so that you are fully prepared. This will also guard against the equally dreadful eventuality of the video not working.

Private reading

This works well with a class of young students but can also be successful with well motivated older students. Basically, it involves them sitting in silence reading a book. You could even plan this for a specific lesson each week, perhaps on a Friday when you (and they) will be tired. The children could bring in their own books related to the subject you are studying. Make sure that you have back-up copies as some students may forget to bring their own books, or may not have access to them. Depending on your viewpoint, and the motivation of the children you teach, you may also feel that it is acceptable for them to read magazines or newspapers during this private reading time.

A library visit

If you are lucky enough to have a good library in your school, and a helpful librarian, you could plan some library visits for your students where you ask them to look up information relating to their work, for instance, for a project. Alternatively, your library may run an induction programme at the start of the school year, and you could book your class into this. One of the basic rules of a library is that the children must be quiet, so this can be very restful for the tired teacher, who will be acting as a supervisor.

Computers

Many schools now have a suite of computers that can be booked by teachers for a class to use. The first few lessons in a computer room will be stressful, particularly if you have to induct and train the children yourself. However, once they are confident about using the computers they will settle quickly to work and will happily stare silently at the computer screens, busily typing away. You can use the chance to visit a computer room as a reward, or build it into a scheme of work, so that you visit on a regular basis, perhaps even once a week.

Remember that there is a wide range of work, not just word processing, that can be accomplished on computers. For instance, in a maths lesson the children could learn how to set up a database; you could do graphics and design work in an art lesson; in a geography class the children could do map-based exercises. There are also many educational programmes available, for instance, on spelling or maths work. The Internet also opens up to your students material on a huge variety of subjects.

Project work

A project on a specific topic area will take a long time to complete and will require the children to work in an independent way. You could allow the students to choose their own activities for the project, or you could provide a list of tasks that they must complete. This works best with a well motivated class, who are able to work on their own. A project can sometimes prove more stressful than it is worth, especially if you have a class who will be constantly going off task. You could combine this project work with visits to the library and the computer room.

Show and tell

Although this is generally regarded as a drama activity, it can be adapted to most subjects. The students spend part of the lesson time preparing a presentation or performance that they then show to the rest of the class. This keeps your involvement to a minimum, and you will have the opportunity to assess their oral work during the lesson.

DEALING WITH DIFFERENTIATION

In my opinion differentiation is rather like close marking (see Chapter 7): all very well in theory, but not always practical for the working teacher. No doubt you will have explored all the types of differentiation at college, and tried them out with your classes. However, you now have a 'real' job and all the extras that come with it: a full timetable, marking to complete, reports to write, forms to fill out, parents' evenings and meetings to attend, and so on. Realistically, you will not be able to differentiate every piece of work you set, unless you are willing to plan and prepare resources until midnight every night. Here, then, are some tips about how you can deal with the need for differentiation:

- *Focus on what really matters*: Because it is simply not possible to differentiate for every single child that you teach, it becomes a matter of focusing your efforts where they will make the most differences. It might be that you have a child in your class who is really struggling because of severe special needs; it could be that you have a small group of students who show a very high level of aptitude for maths or science. Working out where to focus your efforts is an important part of dealing with differentiation.
- *Get help from support teachers*: If you work with a classroom assistant, or with a support teacher of some type, do ensure that you elicit his or her help in differentiating the work. It could be that you create a worksheet, then ask your assistant to develop a simplified version for children who have literacy difficulties.
- *Plan for extension tasks*: It is always the case that a few children will finish work more quickly than others, and this is where extension tasks really come in handy. When you are planning your lessons, always try to organize a few more complex extension activities for those who regularly finish the work early.
- *Develop partnerships amongst your children*: Children can be very good at working together and supporting each other. For instance, it might be that a child who has finished the work set very quickly could, on occasion, offer support and help to a weaker classmate. Helping another student in this way will be beneficial for the children's social skills.
- *Set differentiated homeworks*: For the very brightest children, homework is a time when real progress can be made, because they spend as long as they wish on the tasks. When setting homework, offer a selection of different activities, ranging from

easy to very difficult. You can then offer your children the choice of which ones to complete, or you could specify those students who must work on the hardest tasks.

FINDING RESOURCES

When you start at your school, do check on the resources that are already available. You may find that they are very useful to you and save you replicating work that has already been done. However, you may equally well find that they consist of outdated worksheets or textbooks that are difficult to access and impossible to use effectively.

It could be more useful for you to ask other teachers in your department or area if they have any recently prepared resources on the subjects you are covering. Teachers are usually flattered and keen to offer good material if you are enthusiastic and if you are willing to give your own ideas in return. Do try to present any worksheets you make as effectively as you possibly can, preferably in a typed format and with illustrations. This will encourage the students to use them properly.

Remember too that resources come in many shapes and sizes. Basically, a resource is anything that teachers bring into their lessons to aid the students' understanding of a subject. Students respond particularly well to unusual resources that challenge their creativity and imagination. Here are some ideas for original resources that you could use.

Other teachers

Other teachers can be a very useful resource for you – either the experience and information they can offer which you could use in your lessons, or (if they are willing and they have the free time) they might actually come into your lesson themselves. For instance, you may be a geography or science teacher teaching your students how to draw diagrams, but you may not feel very confident about your own artistic skills. You could ask an art or design teacher to come into your lessons to demonstrate how to make a good technical drawing. You could then offer them an area of specialism of your own in return.

Other adults

It is rare, particularly in secondary schools, for teachers to invite other adults into their classes. This is a shame, as the students will respond very well to someone they have not met before who is an expert, perhaps a poet or an astronomer. Find out if the parents or guardians of your students (or other adults that you know or could approach) are willing to come in and take a lesson or lessons with your class.

As well as bringing in interesting and often exciting information, other adults provide excellent role models for your students. You could find a female bricklayer or a male dressmaker to challenge stereotypes. Other adults can provide important role models for both male and female students. Seeing adults who have other jobs (i.e. other than teachers) can give your students something concrete to aim for beyond the school environment.

In the primary school, teachers can make good use of parental offers of help, for instance, in hearing readers or in helping supervise a school trip. It is always worth asking the parents and guardians of the children in your class if they would be willing to give up some time to help you – you will probably find that they are flattered and delighted to be asked.

Other students

If you have a sixth form in your school, why not approach some of these older students to come and assist you in the classroom? Again, students seem to respond well to non-teachers in the classroom. You could perhaps ask a sixth-former to work with a small group of children, or even one individual who needs extra help and attention. In the primary school, you might organize a group of Year 6 students to work with Year 1 children on practising their reading skills. This cross-school interaction is very helpful for developing many skills outside the traditional curriculum, such as socialization and confidence.

Objects

Children respond very well to a teacher who brings objects, unusual or even common, into the classroom. Of course, science, art and technology teachers use a variety of objects in their lessons, but this is by no means the only time they can be used. For instance, an English teacher working on *Romeo and Juliet* might bring in the 'evidence' found at the murder scene. This would include the poison taken by Juliet, the Friar's letter to Romeo, and so on. The students could then examine the evidence as detectives, and try to work out what has happened. Similarly, a language teacher may obtain a really positive response if they set up a market in the classroom and ask the students to buy different types of food using the correct vocabulary.

In the primary school, teachers do probably tend to use a greater range of props and objects in their daily teaching, especially lower down the school. Here, too, objects have a whole range of interesting possibilities. A jewellery box might become a magic object that holds the key to another world, but which can only be opened by the right spell; a selection of different hats or bags could help you in developing characters for a story.

The library/the Internet

The library and any available CD-ROMs or the Internet are, of course, very useful resources for the students. Embarrassingly, you will probably find that the students are far more at home with the latest technology than you are. Before using ICT resources, it is worth spending some time getting acquainted with the material that is available (either on CD-ROMs or at different websites), so that you can focus your children's work.

USING DISPLAYS

Classroom displays are an essential part of the learning experience for your children: they celebrate the students' work and provide information on a variety of topics. They do take time to prepare and present, but I feel strongly that they are very worthwhile. I would like to offer a few thoughts and ideas about displays for you to consider. Many of these comments are perhaps idealistic – busy teachers will have other things on their minds apart from creating display work. However, it is all part of creating a good working environment for your students and they will respond far better to your lessons (and give you an easier time) if they feel you really care about what they are doing and where they have to work. Consider the following suggestions and comments when creating your own classroom displays:

- *Change the displays regularly*: One of the worst sights in a classroom is a display which is torn, falling down and has graffiti on it. In this instance it would be better for there to be no displays at all. If at all possible, change your displays every half-term, or at least every term. Perhaps use a system of rotation where you always have one class or group working on creating a display and you take down the oldest or tattiest display to make room for the new one. Even if the room is not 'yours', the students will respond very well to seeing that you value their work by displaying it on the wall. They will be proud of it and other groups will probably express an interest in what they have been doing.
- *Avoid 'wallpaper' displays*: This is to say that you should not view displays as 'wallpaper' – something put up to decorate the walls (or hide their condition). In some schools, as an open evening approaches, or as the arrival of inspectors becomes imminent, a frenzy of display work takes place, display work which then stays up for the rest of the school year. However, your students will recognize this type of display for what it is: a promotion of the school rather than for their benefit. Display work should always be a celebration of what is *currently* going on in the classroom. It will take a while for you to fill your walls at the start of term, but this is not a problem.
- *Make it worthwhile*: Only put up work that is worth displaying, perhaps because it is artistically attractive, or because it is worth reading. Try not to put up lots of copies of very similar things, for instance, a whole class worth of the same piece of work. However, do display the work of weaker students, as well as the more able, as this will help motivate them. You could help a student redraft a piece for display if, say, they had a problem with spelling.
- *Interactive displays*: Try and make your displays interactive or even 3-dimensional. This encourages the children to respond to the displays in a positive way. For instance, displays that include questions will invite a response, as will displays that have lift-up flaps. There are many opportunities for creating 3-dimensional displays. In a science lesson you could make models of the

planets and create a solar system; in drama you could get the students to make masks; a teacher working on history could have a display based on fireworks night which includes fireworks made using cardboard rolls. If you don't have any ideas of your own ask an art specialist or the children themselves for some suggestions.

- *By and for the students*: I am all too aware of the temptation to put the displays up yourself, to ensure that they are neat. However, do bear in mind that displays will elicit a more positive response if the students feel that they have created them themselves. If your children are not old enough or capable enough, you could act as an 'artistic director'. By allowing the students to take control, you will also save yourself time. There is no reason why displays should not go up within lesson time, if you have the space to do this.

- *Part of the learning experience*: Always treat a display as part of the children's education. This will happen fairly automatically if it is connected closely to the work they are doing. Do not feel that a display always comes at the end of a topic or subject, as a demonstration of what has been learned. It can also come at or near the beginning of a unit of work, so that you can refer to it during your lessons. Of course, a display can also include pre-printed material. For instance, a map of your local area will be very helpful to a geography class working on a project studying the immediate environment.

- *A motivating factor*: There is something very rewarding about seeing a piece of work that you have done being displayed on a wall for everyone to see. Try putting yourself in the children's shoes and thinking about how good this would make you feel. You will not only motivate the children whose work is on the wall, but also the rest of the class and other children who use or come into the room, as well as pleasing their parents if they come into the classroom.

- *Keep displays tidy*: There is nothing worse than a tatty display, so it is worth taking a few moments whenever you think about it to tidy up the displays in your room. It can be disheartening when students do not treat displays with the respect they deserve, but at least it shows them interacting with the work. By their very nature, displays will become damaged as the students bump into them, so do accept the need to tidy them up on occasion.

TAKING CARE OF YOURSELF

In many ways, teaching is like acting. You are 'performing' to an audience (your children) and you have to be 'in character' as a teacher all (or most) of the time. There will be times when you do not feel like playing your part, but you have no choice – the audience of students are there and waiting for your instructions or your words of wisdom. This can become very tiring; after all, no actor is expected to perform on stage for over 5 hours a day, every day of the week. How, then, can you prevent the inevitable tiredness that you will experience? Here are some ideas to help you avoid and cope with exhaustion during your first year:

- *Take your breaks*: The temptation to work through break-time and lunch is incredibly strong and I can easily see why some teachers do this. You know that the work you have to do (and there is *always* work waiting to be done) will still be there after school, so why not try to get some of it done in your breaks so you can go home earlier? You may have detentions which have to be supervised, or students who need to talk to you about a problem or a piece of coursework. When else are you supposed to do this?

  I would suggest that you are ruthless with yourself about this one. If at all possible, make a point of going for a coffee in the staff room before school starts, getting there during break-time and always having as full a lunch-time as you can. There are two main reasons for this. First and foremost, you need to give yourself the opportunity to rest during the day. You will not serve your students to the best of your ability if you are tired and irritable. Secondly, and perhaps equally importantly, you need to spend time with other teachers. As I pointed out in Chapter 1, the other staff in the school are a vital part of your support system and there is little chance to get to know them unless you go to the staff room. It is also good for you to have some adult company, a chance to have a laugh or a moan. Rest time is *never* wasted time.

- *Take sick leave*: If you are ill, *do not* come into school. I have covered this idea in Chapter 1, but I will happily repeat it. You are not indispensable, you do not want to pass on your illness to other teachers, you *can* afford to take a day off. If you know in advance that you are going to need a day off, for instance, if you feel progressively sicker during the day, then if you really have to, take some marking home with you so you do not get too far behind.

- *Be a quiet teacher*: A musician's tool is an instrument, which can be replaced if it gets broken. You are like an actor – your voice is your tool and you must take care of it, because you only have one and it cannot be replaced. Avoid shouting at all costs, talk as quietly as you can and avoid too much use of the 'chalk and talk' style of teaching, where you are required to talk a great deal. Make your children do the work as often as you can. Remember, 'quiet teachers get quiet classes' (see Chapter 3).

- *Make the most of your holidays*: One of the best perks of a teaching job is undoubtedly the holidays, so use them for the most appropriate reason – to take a break. At the end of term you will feel exhausted, both emotionally and physically. Try to avoid the overwhelming temptation to catch up on all that marking and planning you never have time to do. Remember, your job will expand to fit the amount of time you are willing to devote to it. Be ruthless with yourself and plan lots of lovely holidays (if you can afford them). You will feel better for it.

Chapter 5

Pastoral care

One of the key responsibilities of the teacher, outside of delivering the curriculum, is for the pastoral well-being of his or her children. For the primary school teacher, this pastoral duty will be for the children in the class that you teach. For the secondary school teacher, the pastoral responsibility will be for a form or tutor group. Although at times your pastoral work may seem like just one more burden to cope with during the difficult NQT year, this side of the job is in fact a very rewarding aspect of your role. It will also tend to feed into the teaching and learning that you do with the class, by helping you build up a strong relationship with a particular group of students. This chapter gives you lots of tips and advice about the pastoral side of the job.

YOUR PASTORAL RESPONSIBILITIES

The pastoral responsibilities of the primary teacher or form tutor cover a wide range of areas, including administrative, welfare and social issues. Right from the start of term, you will be in charge of your children's overall welfare and their progress at school. You will have to do jobs such as taking the register, supervising the use of student diaries, helping children new to the school settle in, and so on. All this responsibility can seem quite daunting to the NQT, but it is in fact a very valuable and enjoyable part of a teacher's work. In some secondary schools, NQTs are not allocated a tutor group, or are given a co-tutor with whom they can work while learning the ropes. The sections below give you plenty of advice and suggestions for dealing with the pastoral aspects of teaching.

First-year students

If you have a nursery or reception class, or a first-year (Year 7) form group in a secondary school, your main responsibility at the beginning of term will be to ensure that your children settle in quickly and have all the information that they need. Here is a list of suggestions that will help you prepare for the difficulties you and your students might encounter:

- *Helping the anxious child*: Some of your children may need a lot of reassurance and comforting at the start of term. Starting at primary or secondary school can be a traumatic experience, and you could find yourself acting as a surrogate parent for the first few days and weeks of the academic year. Keep an eye out for any children who are not settling in – this includes the quiet, withdrawn child, as well as those who display their anxiety more openly.
- *Finding their way around*: First-year students will be unsure of the layout of the buildings, and will need help in orientating themselves. Your school should issue you with maps that you can go through with your students. This will also help you in the difficult task of finding your way around. Make sure that the children know the location of the most important areas: the toilets, the class or form room, the assembly hall, the dining room, the student reception, and so on.
- *Understanding the school day*: At first, the timings and arrangements of the school day will be very confusing for new children. They will need to be shown how the timetable works, when breaks take place, how long they are, and so on. One of the biggest changes for students starting at a secondary school is the fact that they have so many different subjects, with a different teacher and a different classroom for each one. Spend time going over lesson changes with your form group right at the beginning of term to ensure that they understand.
- *Using a student diary*: Many schools now use student diaries, so you may need to hand these out and explain to the children how to use them. Make sure you take a good look at one before the term

starts, so that you are aware of exactly what is in it. Go through the different sections of the diary, discussing how it should be used. Ensure that you give the students time to write or stick their timetables into their diaries, so they do not get lost. If you are a form tutor you should receive two copies of each timetable, one to give to the students and one for your own reference.

- *Admin jobs*: There are a whole range of administrative duties that the classroom teacher or form tutor might be asked to perform. For instance, you may find that you have to collect in money for various activities or get details of lunch arrangements. You may also be asked to get your students to fill out an information form, which will give you invaluable details about addresses, names of parents or guardians, telephone numbers, dates of birth, and so on.

Some schools have a staggered start to the first term, so that the new students have a chance to find their feet before the older ones return. You will hopefully get an extended period of time at the beginning of the year so that you can deal with all these additional jobs. If you are a primary school teacher, do not feel that it is vital to rush into the curriculum. If pastoral jobs need doing, allocate some time for this work to be completed first.

Finding out about your students

It can actually be surprisingly difficult, and time-onsuming, to get access to the information you need about your children. When I first started teaching, I had assumed that I might be given a folder with lots of details about my new form group, but in fact I discovered that if I wanted to get hold of information, I often needed to chase it up myself.

- *Contact information*: As mentioned above, you may be asked to get your children to fill in a contact details sheet at the start of term. Alternatively, you may find that this information is written at the front of your register, or that the school office is able to give you any contact details you require.
- *Special educational needs*: Some of your students may have special educational needs (SEN) and it is important that you find out about this as soon as possible. In the secondary school you could talk with special needs staff or with your pastoral manager

who should have material on the students from their previous schools (or, if they are not first years, from previous years at your school). In the primary school, the situation may be more complicated, as many special needs will not yet have been identified.

During the year, you will probably be involved in assessing children in your class who have special needs. This assessment may involve making an initial identification of children who you feel are experiencing difficulties, or simply checking the progress of those already identified as having special needs by looking carefully at their progress in different subjects.

- *Child protection issues*: There could be children in your class or form group who have welfare issues unconnected to their learning. Find out as soon as possible who the designated Child Protection Officer (CPO) is at your school. This person is responsible for dealing with any CP issues. If you do have concerns about a child in your class, talk to the CPO as soon as possible.

The register

Perhaps surprisingly, the register is a legal document, and consequently it is important that you fill it in correctly. Schools now use a variety of different formats for their registers: from the traditional green-covered register, to the computerized SIMs format, to the handheld keypad system. Make sure you get some guidance early on about how to fill in or use your register. You may find that nobody actually offers to go through this with you – if this is the case, please ask! Here are some general points about using your register:

- *Filling in the dates*: If you are lucky, you may find that the office staff at your school have filled in the dates for you in the traditional register. If not, you will need to do this yourself, but you should be very careful not to make a mistake. Ask an experienced member of staff (or someone in the school office) if you are not sure. You should include half-terms and training days in your dates. If your school uses one of the computerized formats, there will be no need for you to worry about filling in dates.

- *Marking present or absent*: When you are taking the register, a student is either absent (shown with a blank or an empty circle) or present (marked with a line). If using a traditional register, check before starting to see what colour pens your school wants you to use in the register. This will probably be black for present and red for absent. With the SIMs format, an HB pencil will normally be used.
- *Absence letters*: When a student has been absent, you must obtain confirmation of this absence from their parents or guardians and a reason for it. In the front of your register (or at the bottom of the SIMs sheet) you will find a list of letters to use for the different types of absence. In the majority of cases, the parents or guardians will send in a letter with the child, but if absence is not authorized almost immediately, you may find it easier to telephone the home. Schools often have a standard letter for you to send home asking the parents or guardians to explain absences.
- *Absence patterns and truancy*: Using your register, watch for any children who display a particular pattern of absence or who are missing a great deal of school. You should also watch for possible cases of truancy. If this happens, or if you have any suspicions, notify your head of year or line manager and the special needs teachers.
- *The register and assembly*: Depending on the size and structure of your school, you will probably have an assembly with your year or class group on at least one day a week. You may be asked to take the register during this assembly. As with your classes, it is very useful to have your students sitting in alphabetical order for this. You will find it much easier to mark them in and you can also start learning their names – a real difficulty if you are a secondary school tutor and you do not actually teach your form group

The student diary

Many schools now use student diaries and these provide a really useful way for communicating with the parents or guardians and with other teachers. Students can write down their homework and other important details in them and teachers can enter detentions, commendations, and so on. Unfortunately, this system is open to abuse: diaries are 'lost' when the detention pages are full; some students manage to get themselves two diaries. The school will usually ask the students' parents or guardians to check the diaries and sign them. Again, although in theory this is a useful device, it is not difficult for the students to perfect a forged signature. Here are some tips about supervising the use of student diaries with your class or form group:

- *Go through the format with the class*: At the start of the year, when diaries are handed out, spend some time going through them with your class. Look at the different sections, talking about what information should be kept in each place. Give your children useful hints about how best to use the diary, for instance, crossing off each homework as it is done.
- *Check them regularly*: Try to have a regular time and day when you check diaries, and stick to this. It is probably best to look over the diaries at least once a week to ensure they are being used properly. This check-up could take place during an assembly if you have one. Make sure you check the detention and rewards pages, as well as ensuring that the parent or guardian has seen and signed the diary.
- *Keep a note of 'lost' diaries*: As I pointed out above, it is not too difficult for the enterprising student to 'lose' a diary full of detentions, or to get hold of a second diary which they then keep 'clean'. A couple of useful ways of deterring this are to charge a fee for each new diary, and to keep a list of who receives one and when.
- *Use the diary as an early warning system*: If a child is receiving a lot of detentions, find a time early on to talk to them about why this is happening. Is there a particular pattern of behaviour developing, or do they appear to have a problem with a specific subject or teacher? If a student is not recording homework in sufficient detail, or does not seem to be set much homework, you should talk to him or her about this as well. It could be that the child is having problems recording the homework.

Contact with parents or guardians

Many primary school teachers, particularly lower down the school, will see the parents or guardians on a more or less daily basis, when they drop the child off at school. If appropriate, this can be the perfect opportunity to have a quick word if you are concerned about a child's progress, or perhaps if behavioural issues are developing. If the start and finish of school are busy times for you, there is no harm in catching the parent and asking to set up an appointment to meet at a more convenient time.

It is often the case that secondary school teachers have very little contact with the student's home, apart from through letters and student diaries. As a form tutor you may well find that you only ever speak to parents or guardians on the phone, or perhaps meet them at parents' evenings. Your school may organize an information evening for new students, and this can be a very worthwhile way of meeting parents or guardians. You will also be communicating with them through subject reports, but at best you can form only a superficial relationship.

Reports

The school report offers an excellent way of communicating with the home, and of showing the parents or guardians how and where their child is progressing (or not). In the primary school, the class teacher will be responsible for reporting on all areas of his or her class's achievement. You will need to comment on the different subjects being studied, as well as on the child's attitude, behaviour, and so on. You can find lots of information and tips on writing reports in Chapter 8.

In the secondary school, one of the most time-consuming aspects of the role of a form tutor comes when reports are due. Tutors are usually responsible for correlating and proofreading all the different subject reports, as well as making their own overall tutor comment about each student's progress. The reason this can take so much time is because you are relying on the commitment and competence of a large number of your colleagues. You may need to have reports sent back and amended, or you may not receive reports at all from some teachers, and you will need to send them reminders. Unfortunately, there is not a great deal you can do about this. Do remember, however, the trouble this causes you and when you are doing reports for other year groups try to hand them in on time and ensure that they are correct the first time around. You will save yourself, as well as other teachers, a lot of time and effort if you do this.

The completed reports will usually be checked by a head of year, a deputy head or other senior manager. They will then be given out to the students, or alternatively posted to the home. You may be asked to obtain return slips from your form, confirming receipt of the report. If there are any children who have proved particularly unreliable (or who have a very poor report that they might not want their parents or guardians to read), it might be best to ensure that the report is posted home, rather than given to the child.

Social and personal issues

One of the most important (and satisfying) parts of being a form tutor is dealing with any social and personal issues that arise with your students. However, dealing with welfare problems can also be very difficult, both for the NQT and for the more experienced teacher. As professionals, we all want the best for the children in our care, and it can be upsetting if we feel they are being ill treated, either at school or in the home. The majority of incidents with which you have to deal will, thankfully, be the more minor ones such as friendships breaking up or name calling. Of course these will often seem very serious indeed to the child involved. Here are some tips about dealing with social and personal issues:

- *Get help with the serious issues*: The more serious issues should always be dealt with in partnership with more experienced or senior teachers. If you do have any suspicions at all about a child's welfare in the home, make sure you refer the situation to your CPO straight away. There will be occasions when a student simply needs to talk to someone about something that is worrying them, and you will need to use your judgement to decide when a higher level intervention is appropriate. If you are at all unsure, don't be afraid to talk with a more experienced colleague about what you should do.
- *Offer an 'open door' policy*: At the start of your time with the class or form group, make it clear that they can come and talk to you privately if they ever need your help. In the primary school you will rapidly develop a very close relationship with each member of your class. In the secondary school, the children may feel closer to a subject teacher, who they spend more time with in school. If a child does decide to approach you for help, always

try and make time to talk to them. If it is not possible for this to happen during registration time, let the child know where you will be at break-time or after school.

- *Provide a shoulder to cry on*: Often a student will just want someone to listen to their problems, a metaphorical or literal shoulder to cry on. You may find your children coming to you about problems in a friendship group, or with minor worries about school or home. Sometimes, all that is required is for you to listen. If you feel that you cannot deal with the child's problem effectively on your own, or if you are concerned that he or she is perhaps depressed or overly anxious, you could refer the child to a school counsellor if you have one.

- *Be a neutral observer*: Try to give your class or form the sense that you care about how they behave in all their lessons and that you really want them to succeed at school. In many ways you can act as a neutral observer and offer them an overview of their behaviour at school, particularly if you are a secondary school form tutor who does not teach the form class. For instance, if one of your students is getting into trouble with teachers because of their confrontational behaviour, you may be able to point this out to them without making them feel angry.

THE ROLE OF THE PASTORAL MANAGER

In the secondary school an experienced teacher will work as head of year or house, managing the form tutors and overseeing the welfare and progress of a large group of children in one year or house group. You should refer any difficult or serious problems to him or her, bearing in mind that a written referral is more helpful than simply having a chat during a spare moment. In this way the manager will have the evidence he or she needs to take the matter further.

You should do the best job you can with your form group, but be careful not to take on extra work that is not really yours, particularly when you are just starting out as a teacher. You may wish to attend any special needs meetings that concern a student from your group, as these will give you additional insight into their problems, but there is normally no compulsion for you to do so. Similarly, if you are experiencing severe difficulties with your form group, perhaps in maintaining reasonable behaviour, do ask your pastoral manager for help and support.

DEVELOPING YOUR ROLE

It really is up to you how far you want to take the pastoral side of your role. In the primary school, because of your close relationship with a single class, you will probably find the curriculum and pastoral aspects of your work intermingling. It is a good idea to develop the sense of your class as a team who are keen to work and learn together, as this will feed into your classroom teaching. In the secondary school you will be spending far less time with your tutor group, but it is still probable that you will develop a strong and lasting relationship with them. There are various ways of motivating your class or form group and making them feel like a team:

- *Competitions*: You might organize a competition to see who can achieve the most merit marks, or whatever reward system your school uses. You may also find that your school runs its own competitions, for instance, to sell tickets to a Christmas market or a noticeboard competition for each year or house group. There might also be competition within or between the classes or form groups to see who has the best attendance and punctuality record.
- *The class/form noticeboard*: A good way to motivate your group and keep them up to date on information is to keep a well organized noticeboard. Depending on the age of the students, they could design and make this themselves, or with your help. The noticeboard could include your name, the name of your form group, a list of the school rules, names of the children in the group, their 'baby pictures', and so on.
- *Special occasions*: An effective way to make your class or form feel that you really care about them would be to give birthday cards, or cards to mark other special occasions such as Christmas or Divali. There are two drawbacks with this idea: the first is that you will have to buy or make the cards yourself, the second is that you must remember to give every single student a card, or they will be very disappointed. Many teachers also give out small presents such as sweets to celebrate the end of term.
- *Admin tasks*: Finally, one of the most time-consuming administrative tasks in a form group is getting them to hand things in, for instance, return slips on reports, absence letters, and so on.

You could motivate them to do this in various ways: one way is to give merits (or some other reward) to those who hand notes in the next day; another way is to give out detentions for those who forget their notes, etc.

Part III

Climbing the Paper Mountain

Chapter 6

Paperwork and marking

When you first start out as a teacher, you will inevitably find it hard
to balance what goes on in the classroom with all the peripheral
aspects of the job. This difficulty applies particularly to paperwork
and marking. Dealing with form filling and marking books can take
up huge quantities of your time outside the classroom, time that
might be better devoted to tasks such as planning and offering
pastoral care. For many NQTs, the paper-based parts of the job can
seem overwhelming. You might find yourself using up huge quantities
of time in a seemingly endless quest to 'finish' that pile of unfilled
forms or unmarked books. Work is taken home on evenings and at
weekends, and stress levels rise as you feel yourself ceasing to have a
life of your own outside the demands of school work. The secret, as
with much of the role of a teacher, is to find a balance that works for
you and your children. This chapter, and the one that follows, will
help you in the difficult job of 'climbing the paper mountain'.

DEALING WITH PAPERWORK

One of the most time-consuming tasks teachers face is to deal with
the mountains of paper that pass through their hands. Of course,
some of this paperwork is important, for instance, reports and SEN
forms. Unfortunately it is also true that the school for which you
work, and the government of the day, will be willing participants in
adding to your paper workload.

How, then, do you deal with this potentially time-wasting aspect of the job? The three rules given below should help you keep the paperwork to a minimum.

The first rule: 'B' is for bin

You should apply this rule to every piece of paper that you receive, and if you follow it as ruthlessly as you can, your pile of important paperwork will stay quite small. The rule goes as follows: as each piece of paper arrives in your pigeon-hole, ask yourself the question, '*Does the thought of throwing this away make me want to cry?*' If the answer is '*No*', then throw it away immediately. If you do make a mistake and throw away something important, someone else will always have a copy.

There are many examples of paper that can end up in the bin. For instance, after reading the agenda for a meeting and attending the meeting itself, there is little point in keeping your copy of the agenda. Similarly, if there is centralized documentation that is easily accessible, you will not need to keep copies of your own. Examples might include department handbooks, duty rotas and so on.

The second rule: File it, deal with it, or pass it on

You should apply this rule to all the paper that you have left over after following the first rule. Once you have weeded out the non-essential paperwork there are three options to consider for what is left: file it, deal with it, or pass it on.

1. *File it*. Be wary of this one. The phrase 'I might use it or need it again' is the way those mountains of paper start to build up. File *only* what is essential (see 'The third rule' below to find out how to decide what to file).
2. *Deal with it*. The best option, faced with any piece of paper that requires a response or action of some type is to deal with it straightaway, as soon as you take it out of your pigeon-hole. That way you can move straight on to option (3) with the leftovers. If you don't feel confident about dealing with it, check immediately with somebody else what you should do. If you feel the piece of paper requires a more considered response, by all means take your time, but avoid having a pile of papers known as 'to be done'. When, exactly, are you going to 'do' them?

3. *Pass it on.* Always the preferred option, as it ensures your paperwork becomes somebody else's problem. Whenever possible, for instance, when filling out special needs forms, do not agonize about what you are going to write. Fill the form in that instant and then pass it on. It is far better to do this than to be one of those teachers with piles of forms that they will *never* fill in on their desks. If you do it wrong the first time nobody is going to blame you; you have only just started teaching after all, and they can always come back to you if it does need changing.

The third rule: Will I use it again?

Finally, the third rule deals with everything left over after you have followed Rules (1) and (2). Just be honest with yourself. If you have made a photocopiable resource, keep a copy, but make sure it is easily accessible. If it is not, you will end up making it again at some point in the future, so what is the point in keeping it? If you can, file one copy of each worksheet in a plastic folder that you can take out easily to photocopy. When filing, it is useful to have your resources divided into different topics and also into different year groups.

If you have access to a computer of your own, this is the ideal way to store your resources, as it makes searching for and printing them out a very simple task. However, be wary of storing resources on a school computer: they may well disappear or at the very least get lost among the work of other teachers. If you do use a computer at school, set up a folder of your own in which to store your work.

MARKING: A BALANCING ACT

Marking is, like many aspects of teaching, a job that expands to meet the amount of time you are willing (or able) to devote to it. On teaching practice, it is likely that your timetable was only a fraction of that of a full-time teacher and you had plenty of (or at least enough) time for planning and checking your students' work. Now you have to deal not only with teaching and marking, but also with all the other administrative tasks that come with the job, including writing reports and attending meetings. It is now that you find out just how much of a balancing act marking really is.

You might have heard complaints from those outside the teaching profession that teachers 'do not bother' to correct mistakes in their students' work. This, of course, is not necessarily true. It is more likely a result of the fact that close marking (see the following section in this chapter) takes a great deal of time. If a teacher were to close mark a three-page piece of work, adding lots of comments and corrections, it could take up to half an hour (depending on the subject being marked). Multiply this by an average of 25 or 30 students in a class, then by the number of subjects or classes the teacher has to teach and you can see why this is practically impossible. Teachers may have a shorter working day than other professionals, but a marking load of over 100 hours a week is not realistic.

Teachers have to make difficult decisions about marking. Some of these are listed below:

- *Balancing marking with other parts of the job*: Early on, you will need to decide how you are going to balance the importance of checking your children's work with the equal necessity to plan lessons, make resources, create displays, and so on. There are no hard and fast rules to follow, and it is tempting to feel that the books must 'appear' to be marked. It is well worth questioning for yourself the value of the various different marking methods for your children's educational achievement.

- *Deciding on your priorities*: For the primary teacher, decisions will need to be made about marking in the different subjects, and whether some areas have priority over others. For the secondary teacher, it is a case of deciding which classes are most important at any one time: for instance, coursework from an examination year class needs to be checked carefully.

- *Keeping a home/work balance*: Generally speaking, there is no realistic way that you can complete close and detailed marking at school and so you must decide whether you are willing to spend evenings and weekends finishing it. At the same time, you must ensure that your work life does not take over your home life.

THE OPTIONS

Teachers are, of course, individuals who mark work in a wide variety of ways. The marking style you choose also depends very much on the age range and subject you are teaching. When you first start teaching you will probably want to experiment with different methods to see how effective you find each one. Your choice of how to mark will depend, too, on your educational philosophies, the policies of your department or school, and how much time you are willing to spend. However, before you start it is worthwhile exploring a few of the options.

Pencil or pen?

There are various different opinions on this, but your school or department will probably have a specific policy that they ask you to follow. I recommend that you question the value of each option and make your own decision. The main points to consider are as follows:

- *Pencil*: Pencil marks are easier to change if you make a mistake but they are harder for the child to see and more vulnerable to alteration. Using a pencil suggests that the teacher's comments or grades are only a subjective judgement rather than a definitive one: the child is not necessarily right or wrong, but the teacher is giving an opinion of the work. This is particularly useful in subjects where the work is imaginative rather than factual. Pencil can be a very useful way of marking important pieces of work, for instance, final drafts of examination coursework, as the student can make necessary alterations using correction fluid and then rub out the pencil marks.
- *Pen:* Pen marks are easier for the child to see, but harder for you to change if you make a mistake. Student alterations are practically impossible, although I have seen it done. Using a pen gives a stronger suggestion that the teacher is judging the child's work and is therefore perhaps more suited to subjects that have right and wrong answers. Some students actually feel more comfortable with pen marks, as they *want* the teacher to make a definitive judgement on their work.

Grading your students

Your choice of whether to use marks, letters, numbers or comments (or a combination) will depend on your school or departmental policies, on the subject that you are teaching and on your own personal marking philosophy. In many instances you will want to give a final grade of some type on a piece of work, simply so that you can keep a record of how each child is doing. In some situations, though, it may be better to simply make a brief comment on the work that highlights areas of achievement, and pinpoints strategies for further improvement. The thoughts below give an overview of the considerations involved in grading your students:

- *Using definitive marks*: In many subjects, or for particular pieces of work, it will be possible to give a definitive mark. For instance, a series of maths sums or a spelling test can be given a mark out of a total score, or an essay could be graded to show whether it is of A, B, C standard and so on. Many students do like to have a definitive mark that shows the level at which they are working in relation to others, and in relation to statutory requirements (for instance, in SATs or GCSE exams).

- *Comparing results*: Giving a definitive mark allows the teacher to compare results. You might wish to check each child's progress from one week to the next and a series of definitive marks or grades will help you do this. Alternatively you might want to check progress across the class as a whole.

- *Grading across year groups*: If you are a secondary school teacher, you will need to find out whether you are supposed to grade pieces of work in relation to the student, the group, or the year as a whole. For instance, is a grade A in a bottom set the equivalent to a grade A in a top set?

- *The potential for demoralizing the weak*: One of the biggest problems with giving out definitive grades or marks is that they can be very offputting for the child who is struggling. If one of your weakest students tries really hard on a particular piece of work, but still produces very poor results, do you really want to demoralize him or her by giving a very low grade? This problem can be avoided somewhat by giving two grades, one for effort and one for attainment.

- *Honesty vs diplomacy*: You will also have to come to a decision about how ruthless you are going to be about grading students (both on class work and reports). If a grade E is the lowest grade you can give, and on the report is explained as 'very poor quality of work' or a similarly negative comment, how willing are you going to be to give a child this grade? There is a real dilemma here between being honest (and alerting parents or guardians and special needs teachers to any problems) and destroying a student's confidence.

Tick and flick

This type of marking is exactly as it sounds: a big tick (or cross) on each answer, then move on to the next. At the end of the work there may be a brief comment, such as 'good' or 'a fair attempt', and a grade or mark. Certain subjects or particular pieces of work may demand this type of marking: for instance, a series of maths sums or a test on vocabulary learned in language lessons.

In some cases, though, this would not be the appropriate style of marking. For instance, a piece of creative writing or a long and detailed essay could be marked in this way, but it would be a fairly meaningless exercise and would have little value for the student. Similarly, if it was clear that a child doing a maths test had not understood the work, you would probably want to write comments and give examples to show where he or she was going wrong.

Close marking

This is what some people see as the ideal (but, as I have explained, an unrealistic ideal in the majority of cases). In close marking the teacher pinpoints and corrects every error. There are obviously advantages in this method, not least of which is that the child sees exactly where he or she is going wrong. However, for weaker students this style of marking can be extremely destructive. If a student has worked hard on a piece which is then covered in red ink this would be very demoralizing.

Marking for specific errors

As well as offering a good balance between 'tick and flick' and close marking, this marking approach also encourages the students to focus on correcting their work themselves. With this style of marking the teacher pinpoints one area for which he or she will be marking. Examples would include: the correct spelling of certain words (you could give a list out beforehand); the proper use of punctuation in a piece of writing; showing detailed working (even if the answers are wrong); producing neat diagrams; correct use of technical terminology, and so on. This encourages the student to concentrate on areas of weakness and you can also set different marking targets for different children, depending on their specific problems.

SOME TIME-SAVING TIPS

There is a real temptation to think of marking as something the teacher does after a lesson, for the children to look through and absorb when a piece of work is returned to them. However, there are some very good ways of saving time with marking that are actually very sound educationally speaking. The strategies given below offer you some time-saving tips to help you cope with your marking load. The majority of them require the students to have a reasonable level of skill in reading and writing, so are more suited to the upper end of the primary school or at secondary level.

Do-it-yourself

Before you collect in a piece of work, or if a few of your students finish the work you have set early, ask them to check through their work themselves. If you know a child has problems in one area, you could ask him or her to look for a specific type of mistake, for instance, to underline any words that might have been misspelt, or circle any technical terms that are wrongly used. When the work has been checked through, you could ask the child to look up the correct spellings in a dictionary as an extension activity.

Do-it-together

This is very useful if you are setting a test where the answers are straightforward and can be marked as right or wrong. After the test has finished you go through the answers one by one with the class, perhaps writing them on the board, and ask your students to tick (or cross) their work and give a mark at the end. If it is important that the results are accurate, you could ask the children to swop with a partner to guard against cheating.

What's your opinion?

This technique is useful for pieces of work that call for an opinion rather than a mark, for instance, art and design or creative writing. In my experience, although they might moan about this exercise at first, the children actually really enjoy it. When the time for completing a piece of work is up, you ask a few students to collect all the books or papers in and 'shuffle' them, then return them to the class, ensuring that no one gets their own work to mark. For this exercise you should give the students specific areas to mark and you should also let them know what you want the marks to be out of. For instance, you could ask for marks out of 10 for creativity, accuracy, originality, and so on. You could also ask them to write a positive comment saying what they liked about the work.

If anyone finishes early, or if you have time, get a second (and third) set of marks and comments from your students by asking them to swop again. They should then return the work to its owner who can read what his or her peers have put. Students tend to take this exercise seriously, as they like playing the role of teacher and when you collect the work in you will have a ready-made set of comments to assist your own marking. Your students will also learn valuable lessons about the standard of work that their peers are producing, and this can be a good motivating factor for those who are producing lazy or sloppy work.

Marking in class

In some situations it is possible to mark work in class, perhaps if students are finishing an exercise at different rates or if they are working in silence on a test and you can be sure that they won't start talking or cheating the minute you lower your head. I have found that it is difficult to get any meaningful marking done during lesson time because there are so many interruptions. However, if you do find it possible it will certainly save you some time.

Remember that in some subjects your marking is not just of written pieces, but of oral work as well. You could ask your students to prepare a presentation on a topic during the lesson that you can watch and assess (see Chapter 4, p. 70, 'Lessons for the tired teacher'). This exercise takes time and is also student-intensive, rather than teacher-intensive, so it will give you the opportunity to have a rest.

COLLECTING WORK

As I suggested in Chapter 1, you should always ask your children to collect in the work for you unless there is a specific reason not to do so, as this will save you time and effort and they will be perfectly willing to help. If you are collecting in homework, one way to ensure that everyone has completed the task you set is to ask the students to have their books in front of them, open at the page where they have done the homework. You can then go around and check that everyone has completed the task, before the books are collected in. Any students who have not completed the homework should have their diaries out, so that you can write in the detention or other sanction they have earned.

There is some discussion about when it is best to collect in homework but really it depends very much on the class. If there are going to be confrontations about uncompleted homework, you might be best to wait until the end of the lesson rather than risk disruption, but do make sure you leave yourself time to write down the names of those who need to be sanctioned. Alternatively, once the children have settled down to work you could go around checking homework and giving out punishments or reprimands. Don't forget to also hand out rewards to those who have completed their work to a good standard.

KEEPING MARKS

It is important to keep a record of the marks that your students achieve, so that when you come to write reports or attend a parents' evening, you have the information at hand. (Inspectors will also want to see detailed information about grades and marks.) It is very much a matter of personal taste how you do this, but I would suggest that rather than have a separate mark book you keep them in your teacher's planner (see Chapter 2). For the secondary school teacher, with a number of different classes, the marks could be kept on a separate page to the class register, but in the same section as the class they relate to. The reason for this is so that you have a line of marks for each student that give an immediate overview of progress (or lack of it). Because they are in the same place as your register, it will be easy to verify whether a student was present or absent from the lesson when checking off homework.

Chapter 7

Exams and reports

This chapter deals with the more formalized types of paper-based work and assessment that you must do. You can find information here about helping your children to prepare for and take exams, and lots of tips and ideas on how to write reports. I also give a list of useful phrases for report writing that you should be able to use to save you some time. In recent years, formalized assessment and reporting do seem to have become a far more central part of our education system, and it's an important area for the new teacher to become acquainted with.

EXAMS AND THE NQT

Preparing your children for examinations can be a rather daunting task for the NQT. Obviously, taking (and hopefully passing) exams is a very important part of your students' education. There may be substantial pressure from the managers at your school, as well as from the parents or guardians, for you to ensure good results. The information, thoughts and ideas that follow should help you in keeping the nerves at bay, and in getting your children ready to do as well as they can.

Statutory exams

Statutory exams are those exams which are taken by all children at a specific point in their schooling, and which are set (and mainly marked) by external bodies. The government of the day decides on the stage at which these assessments take place. In recent years the trend has been towards ever increasing statutory assessment of school children.

Whether or not your children face statutory exams during your first year of teaching will depend on the age range you are teaching, and the particular age group or groups with whom you work. As you will see from the list below, a series of externally assessed exams now take place at frequent intervals during a child's school career:

- Year 2 – SATs
- Year 6 – SATs
- Year 9 – SATs
- Year 11 – GCSEs, NVQs
- Year 12 – AS levels
- Year 13 – A levels

In addition to the exams which are sat under timed conditions, many of the statutory assessments also involve a measure of teacher input. This might take the form of a classroom assessment that the teacher must grade, it could be that the students must complete coursework or modular assessments over the course of the examination year. It is this aspect of the statutory exams that can mean an addition to your paperwork and marking load.

School exams

Even if your children do not face statutory exams in your NQT year, you will find that many schools do have a period for school exams during the academic year. These usually take place towards the end of the academic year, in the summer term. These school exams can have quite an impact on your paperwork levels, as the marking load can be substantial.

SOME TIPS ON EXAMS

The tips that follow give you lots of advice about how to get your students ready for their exams, whether these are statutory ones or within the school. Although I would not advocate actually 'teaching to the tests', it is only fair to help your students prepare as much as possible in advance of their exams, particularly if they are statutory ones.

Preparing your students

Many children feel very nervous in the run-up to the examination period, and you can help them fend off this feeling by keeping them well informed about what exactly to expect. The tips below will help you prepare your children for the big event:

- *Be well informed*: It is important that you prepare your children for the specific tests or syllabus that they are doing, whether these are internal school exams or externally assessed statutory tests. Take the time to check carefully and well in advance what they must do, and to prepare your class for what is going to happen. This might mean time spent reading National Curriculum requirements, past papers, mark schemes, and so on. It might simply mean doing some activities that are similar to those that will be set in the school exams.
- *Get help if you need it*: With a few years' experience, helping your students prepare for their exams becomes second nature. However, at this stage you may well need some help and advice, so don't be ashamed to admit that you're not exactly sure what you are meant to be doing. If you are uncertain about any aspects of the preparation or the exams themselves, do ask a more experienced member of staff, perhaps your induction tutor, for assistance.
- *Get acquainted with past papers*: One of your top priorities, if you are teaching an examination year, is to look closely at the past papers (whether these are SATs papers, GCSEs, etc.). As you look at these past papers, think about the following, and communicate the relevant information to your children:
  - how the paper is laid out;
  - what timing applies to each section or question;
  - what marks apply to each question;
  - whether specific, similar questions come up each time;
  - whether certain topics tend to be repeated.
- *Do lots of practice*: Spend lots of time getting your children to take mock exams, either practical or written depending on your subject. This is important because it will train them to work

quickly – one of the most useful skills in an examination – and also because it will show them just how hard (and long) exams can be. They must also learn to get the timing right – point out to them that the examiner will give marks for each answer and if they do not finish the paper they will not gain any marks for the uncompleted sections.

- *Teach exam technique:* As an adult who has come through exams of your own, you will know all about the best techniques for doing well in exams, so share this information with your children, however young or old they are. For instance, try to persuade them not to 'waffle' or to give unnecessary detail. Passing exams is often a case of simply answering the questions clearly and concisely. There is a great temptation for students to feel that the more they write, the better they will do.

Coursework

In the secondary school, external examinations (depending on the syllabus you are studying and the subject you are teaching) may well be made up of coursework and a final paper or papers. If coursework does play a part in your syllabus, ask your head of department for advice and find out the deadlines for handing in essays or projects. You may find that some of your students have difficulty in completing coursework, but bear in mind that something is better than nothing and even if they have not managed to complete a finished piece of work, you should still be able to find something to enter. A student will often be withdrawn from the exam if they do not enter all the coursework required.

Marking coursework, whether the first drafts or the final product, can take up a great deal of your time. This is especially true if you need to write detailed comments on the coursework to show how and where you have allocated marks. If possible, it is a good idea to get your students to hand in their coursework before the date it is actually required, giving them an artificially early deadline. This helps guard against problems with coursework not being handed in on time, and you may also be able to start your marking early.

What to bring to the exams

Do ensure that your students know exactly what they must bring to their exams, whether this is simply a pencil and ruler, or if it includes more complex technical equipment. If the exam allows them to take in additional aids, then make sure that they do so: a calculator to the maths exam; a dictionary to the languages exam; copies of set texts to the literature exam. Any student who does not have access to this equipment will be severely disadvantaged.

How to pass exams

Passing (or failing) exams can be as much to do with how the child approaches the exam, as to do with the actual ability of the student. It might be tempting to assume that our children know how to approach and pass their exams, but in reality this is not necessarily the case. It really is worth training your students in the skills they will need to pass and do well in their exams. Here are some useful pointers about the type of training you might give:

- what and how to revise;
- any necessary preparatory work;
- how to use the time effectively, both in revision and in the exams themselves;
- any skills specific to the subject, for example, how to write essays, how to draw clear diagrams, how much working to show in analytical answers, etc.

INVIGILATION

Think of the most boring thing you can imagine in the whole world, multiply it by 20, and you have some idea of how boring invigilation is. The summer arrives and you think: *'Great, things are a bit quieter at this time of year, at last I'll be able to catch up on all that paperwork.'* Think again. Now is the time of year when any free lessons (i.e. those frees created by classes on study leave or by children taking exams) are likely to be taken up by invigilation. You must stand in the hall or gym (or wherever the exams are taking place) and watch a large group of students for the duration of your normal lesson time. You cannot do marking or planning during this time, but are required to walk up and down the rows, checking that the students are not cheating, handing out paper and answering any queries.

Some of the more imaginative teachers I have met come up with various ways of making time pass quickly, and I shall leave it to you to see how inventive you can be. One word of warning: although it is rare to see members of the senior management invigilating (they *know* how boring it is, and anyway, they are far too busy running the school), you may find that from time to time the head or a deputy head pops in to see how the students (and teachers) are doing. At this point, you should make a determined effort to look really engrossed in the thrilling task of invigilation. Good luck!

SOME TIPS ON WRITING REPORTS

Reporting to parents and guardians takes many different forms: from an informal chat on the telephone to the more formalized written reports and parents' evenings. Schools use a very wide range of formats and styles for their written reports. Some use a computerized bank of statements for each subject from which the teacher can choose; some use a combination of tick boxes or statements for specific subject skills alongside a written teacher comment; others require the teachers to devise comments of their own. The ideas and suggestions in this and the following two sections will be of most use to teachers who have to provide their own statements. If your school uses a computerized format for their reports, you could look through the phrases given in 'Some useful phrases for reports' and ask your manager or head of department to add some of them to your own bank of comments. Here are some initial thoughts about the whole report-writing process:

- *It's very time-consuming!*: In my first year as a teacher, I was amazed to discover just how time-consuming preparing, writing and collating reports actually is. As you settle into your first term at school, be wary of the feeling that the workload is not actually as bad as you expected – what this probably means is that report-writing has not yet started!
- *A clear form of communication*: Reports are not some kind of essay written for your college lecturer's approval, they need to communicate your thoughts to a whole range of different parents and guardians, and must be written as clearly and concisely as you can.
- *It needs to look and sound professional*: The report is one of the

main forms of communication between the school and the home. You should therefore make sure that you present it neatly and think carefully about what you are going to say. Your school will have its own rules for written reports, but generally you will find that you are required to write in black ink rather than blue, and that you are not allowed to use correction fluid on your reports (see the following section for short cuts here). Remember, a member of the senior management may check your reports, so ensure that you make a good impression.

- *Strategies, targets and progress*: A good report will include strategies for improvement and some specific targets for the student to focus on: words such as 'aim', 'ensure', 'develop', and so on are useful here. As well as setting targets for improvement, it is also important that you give the parents or guardians honest information on how the student is progressing.

- *The need to be positive*: Do try to stress the positive in your reports. This means phrasing what you write in such a way as to encourage, rather than demotivate, the child. For instance, a negative, poorly written report (although rather over-exaggerated) might say: '*Johnny can't concentrate for longer than a few minutes and he's always ruining my lessons by chatting to his mates.*' A more positive version of this, which also incorporates some targets for the student, could say: '*Although he tries hard, Johnny does find it difficult to maintain his concentration for extended periods of time. He should aim to avoid being distracted by other students in the class.*'

- *Achieving a balance*: There will be occasions where you find it almost impossible to say anything positive about a student. Do bear in mind that a child who is proving this difficult to teach will be (or should be) receiving help from special needs teachers. Unless you feel very strongly about having your say, do try to be positive in the way that you phrase your report. The parents or guardians, and indeed the student, will no doubt be used to receiving very negative comments. This may well lead to even greater alienation from school. The key is to achieve a balance between honesty and subtlety.

In 'Some useful phrases for reports' below you will find a list of phrases that you may find helpful when you come to write your reports. I would also strongly urge you to put at least one personalized comment on each report. As you will see from the comments there is no need to use overly technical or complicated language, indeed, you should avoid doing this if possible. The recipients of the report will come from a variety of backgrounds and will all need to understand what the teacher is saying. You should therefore avoid unnecessarily complicated vocabulary, as well as avoiding the use of slang and abbreviations.

SHORT CUTS TO WRITING REPORTS

As I mentioned above, report-writing really is a very time-consuming process. I would, however, urge you very, very strongly to hand in your reports on time. The date that reports will be received by parents and guardians is written into the school timetable, and it would be very embarrassing indeed to have to admit that your own reports are going to be late. In the primary school, it is likely that your reports will be checked by a more senior member of staff, and you will be keen to make a good impression. In the secondary school there is nothing more infuriating (or unprofessional, for that matter) than to have to chase a teacher for a set of reports that should have been handed in the previous week. The names of teachers who never file their reports on time will be well known in your staff room. Do not add your name to the list!

In order to help you avoid this, there are some short cuts you can take, which should not affect the quality of your reports too greatly. These short cuts are particularly applicable to the secondary school teacher who sees lots of different classes in one year group. If you are working at primary level, or if you teach a secondary subject where you see the students a few times a week, you should be able to give rather more individualized reports, and I would recommend that you do so. Although reports are obviously important, there is (and always will be) a great variation in the quality of different subject reports in a secondary school. You will have to balance your desire for the students' parents or guardians to feel that you are a very caring and efficient teacher, with the need to get the reports done (and handed in) in a realistic amount of time. Do not beat yourself up about using the following short cuts if they prove necessary:

- *Start well in advance*: In some secondary subjects the teacher faces the prospect of writing reports on students that they may not know at all well. The teacher may only see each class once a week, for instance, with a subject like music, drama or art, and this will make identifying (let alone assessing) the students a nightmare. You may find that you teach five classes in a particular year group, and when report time comes around you have approximately 150 different reports to write. Do try to plan in advance for this eventuality and start these reports as early as you can. Remember, even if your school uses a computerized format, it will still take you a long time to choose comments and print out the reports.

- *Use 'types' of student*: A good short cut is to group your students into types, basically the weakest, the average and the good. You could stretch this to five categories if you wanted to include those with special problems and the really excellent students. You should then find three or four general statements that cover each of these categories, giving one personalized statement for each student. This would be particularly easy to do if your school does use the computerized bank of statements.

- *Use a computer*: Even if you are asked to devise your own reports, access to a computer can greatly speed up the process, as you can feed each category of reports through the printer. Simply take your general statements, add one personal one at the beginning, and print them out. Do be careful, however, that you have not made any mistakes in your general statements. If you have, you will have to reprint or correct the whole set. Be careful, also, to change the gender on the report as appropriate.

- *If you have to handwrite*: When producing handwritten reports, always use a black pen, preferably one that can be photocopied without losing definition. If you do not have access to a computer, then why not ensure that your writing is on the large side and that your signature takes up as much of the page as is feasible?

- *Use tick boxes*: If your school or department does not already do so, try suggesting tick boxes for different subject skill areas. You could then add just one or two comments on the end of the report, rather than having to comment on the skills in full.

SOME USEFUL PHRASES FOR REPORTS

The following phrases should prove applicable to most age ranges and subjects, as they give generalized comments about the sort of skills a student needs to succeed in his or her lessons, i.e. attitude, behaviour, concentration, etc. You will, of course, want to add your own subject-specific comments, for instance, on factual knowledge, reading and writing skills, analytical ability, creativity, and so on. I have grouped the phrases into the categories given in the previous section which range from 'special problems' to 'really excellent' students. I have also provided some personalized comments that I might use as appropriate and a model report for each category of student. In this model report I omit any subject comments that you would, of course, need to include.

Students with special problems

Approach/attitude:

- Finds it very hard to take a positive approach to lessons.
- Needs to develop a more positive attitude towards this subject.

Behaviour:

- Has found great difficulty in maintaining suitable behaviour in class.
- Must ensure that he/she avoids disruptive or confrontational behaviour.

Concentration:

- It is essential that he/she develops his/her ability to concentrate for extended periods of time.
- Must aim to focus on the task in hand at all times.

Co-operation:

- Must learn to co-operate with the other students in the class.
- Must ensure that he/she treats other students with respect at all times.

Communication skills:

- Needs to learn to communicate clearly and effectively.
- Must ensure that he/she listens carefully at all times.

Contributions to the class:

- Must learn to contribute constructively to the class.
- Should always value the contributions of other students.

Homework:

- Is having difficulty completing homework tasks on time.
- Must ensure that homework is completed to the best of his/her ability.

A model report

John has found it very hard to settle into this class. (*Personal comment which hints at, rather than states, the fact that John is a difficult and anti-social student.*) Although he does try his best, he finds it difficult to behave well. John must approach his lessons in a positive way and treat other students properly. If he is to make progress in this subject, he must learn to concentrate better. John must also complete all homework on time and as well as he can.

Weak students

Approach/attitude:

- Needs to develop a more consistent approach to this subject.
- Should aim to take a positive attitude to his/her lessons.

Behaviour:

- Should aim to behave in an appropriate manner at all times.
- Is working towards improving his/her behaviour in lessons.

Concentration:

- Needs to learn to maintain concentration for extended periods of time.
- Should concentrate fully on the tasks set.

Co-operation:

- Should be more willing to co-operate with all members of the class.
- Should treat other students with respect at all times.

Communication skills:

- Should aim to make more contributions to class discussions.
- Needs to listen more carefully to instructions.

Contributions to the class:

- Should aim to contribute his/her ideas on a more regular basis.
- Must listen carefully to the contributions of other students.

Homework:

- Should ensure that homework is completed to the best of his/her ability.
- Must hand all homework in on time.

A model report

Candice takes a positive approach to this subject but her enthusiasm can result in a lack of concentration. (*Personal comment which suggests that Candice is normally a good student but can lose focus at times.*) She finds some aspects of this subject difficult, but is trying hard to improve. Candice should ensure that she treats other students with respect at all times. She should also make sure that she completes all homework tasks set to the best of her ability. This will help her to develop in those areas of this subject which she finds hard.

Average students

Approach/attitude:

- Usually takes a positive approach to this subject.
- Has a positive attitude that he/she should aim to build on further.

Behaviour:

- Is generally well behaved during lessons.
- Is a quiet and polite student, who always behaves appropriately in class.

Concentration:

- Is working hard to develop his/her concentration.
- Should aim to concentrate for increasing periods of time.

Co-operation:

- Co-operates well with other members of the class.
- Is willing to work in a variety of different groups.

Communication skills:

- Offers some ideas to the class and should now aim to be more confident.
- Listens well to instructions.

Contributions to the class:

- Makes interesting contributions to class discussions.
- Listens well to what other students have to say.

Homework:

- Always hands his/her homework in on time.
- Completes all homework tasks set to a fair standard.

A model report

Fred is usually a hard-working student who is always polite and well behaved in class. (*Personal comment which suggests that Fred is a fairly good student who behaves well, but could probably do better.*) He tries his best even when he finds the work difficult and always listens well to instructions. Fred should now aim to become more confident when contributing to class discussions and to complete all homework tasks set to the best of his ability.

Good students

Approach/attitude:

- Is a keen student who always takes a positive approach to lessons.
- Has an excellent attitude towards this subject.

Behaviour:

- Is always polite and well behaved in class.
- Sets a good example to other students by his/her behaviour.

Concentration:

- Can maintain a good level of concentration for extended periods.
- Shows good concentration when working individually.

Co-operation:

- Works very well with all the other students in the class.
- Is a co-operative student who always shows respect for others.

Communication skills:

- Always listens carefully to instructions.
- Offers some very interesting ideas in lessons.

Contributions to the class:

- Is always willing to make contributions to discussion work.
- Makes interesting and helpful contributions to the class.

Homework:

- Always completes homework tasks on time and to a high standard.
- Has produced some excellent homework assignments.

A model report

Kelly is a great asset to the class. She always approaches lessons in a positive way and shows a real talent for this subject. (*Personal comment that should please both Kelly and her parents/guardians. It is always encouraging for a student when a teacher suggests that they have a 'talent' for a subject.*) She has worked hard to improve her work and is a keen participant in lessons. She should now aim to become more confident about contributing her ideas to the class. It is a pleasure to teach such a hard-working student.

Excellent students

Approach/attitude:

- Is a keen and conscientious student who is always willing to participate.
- Maintains an excellent attitude in every lesson.

Behaviour:

- Has maintained his/her excellent standard of behaviour.
- Sets an excellent example for other students in the way he/she behaves.

Concentration:

- Can maintain excellent concentration for extended periods of time.
- Demonstrates a high level of concentration at all times.

Co-operation:

- Is always willing to co-operate and help other students.
- Shows excellent leadership skills during group work.

Communication skills:

- Communicates his/her ideas in a confident and eloquent way.
- Listens very carefully at all times and asks highly perceptive questions.

Contributions to the class:

- Has made some fascinating contributions to discussion work.
- Is a very valuable member of the class.

Homework:

- Is always beautifully presented with a high standard of content.
- Has completed some impressive homework assignments.

A model report

It is a pleasure to teach Jasdeep. He is an extremely conscientious student and he is producing work of an exceptionally high standard. (*Personal comment that suggests just how good Jasdeep is at this subject and also praises his approach.*) He sets an excellent example for other students in the way he behaves and he is always willing to co-operate with and help the other members of the class. His homework is always beautifully presented with an excellent standard of content. He should aim to continue working as he has been doing so far. Well done, Jasdeep!

Some personalized comments

- Is always polite and hard-working in class.
- Is a lively student with a very positive attitude.
- Is a very valuable member of the class.
- Shows a real talent for this subject.
- Is keen, conscientious and always willing to help.
- Has a very mature attitude.
- Is a real pleasure to teach.
- Is a talented student who should aim to fulfil his/her potential.

Part IV

It's All About People

Chapter 8

Students

Teaching is, of course, all about working with the students (whether they are toddlers, children, young people, teenagers, or adults). In this chapter, you'll find lots of advice and information about dealing with different children. There's information about developing good relationships with your students, ideas for helping those with special needs, case studies based on a range of different types of student, and many other helpful hints and strategies.

YOU AND YOUR STUDENTS

Being a teacher is all about creating, developing and sustaining relationships with the children and young people with whom we work. If we cannot create a positive and respectful relationship with each and every child, it is unlikely that we are going to encourage our students to achieve their best. Here are some initial thoughts about the relationship between you and your children:

- *It takes time*: Although it would be wonderful if our children instantly bonded with us and respected us, in reality it can take a great deal of time before a strong relationship is achieved. This is perhaps especially so for the secondary school teacher with a large number of different classes and students. Don't expect miracles – it could be a year or more before some of your children come round to you.
- *Fear vs respect:* A teacher who is feared by his or her classes may

well receive good behaviour, but in the long run there is little chance of a real and reciprocal relationship being developed. On the other hand, the teacher who is respected by the children will have a far stronger relationship which is likely to be much more educationally valuable.

- *A two-way street*: You might do all that you possibly can for your children, and still find it impossible to break through the barriers that some of them put up. Do bear in mind that creating relationships is a two-way street – some of your students, for instance, those from a difficult or aggressive background, may find it almost impossible to show you the same respect that you give them.
- *You might not like them all*: It is a fact of life that we don't necessarily like every person with whom we come into contact. It can be very difficult for teachers when they work with a child whom they don't like all that much, particularly in the primary classroom where you are stuck with one class for a whole year. You might find yourself feeling guilty at your negative emotions towards a particular student, but in reality you are simply being human. So long as your emotions are not apparent in the way that you treat your students, and you offer each and every individual a fair and equal chance, you are doing the best that you possibly can.
- *Dealing with the poorly behaved*: It is likely that the majority of students you encounter will be well adjusted and keen to work. However, most teachers will also have to face children who have behavioural problems (which may or may not be related to a special educational need). As a professional, it is your duty to deal with these individuals in the best way that you possibly can, and to ensure that they have full access to a good education. You will also have to make sure that their behaviour does not jeopardize the education of the other students in your class, and this is often harder than it sounds.
- *Special educational needs*: When you collect your class lists you may receive information about those students with special educational needs. You will need to find out, preferably before you start teaching, just what the needs of the students in your groups are. Details of the abbreviations commonly used for SEN are given in 'Special educational needs' later in this chapter and in Chapter 11.

- *Don't prejudge your children*: Try to avoid having preconceptions about your children based on what other teachers might say about them, or on the information you receive about their special needs. Students who have behavioural problems in some classes or subjects, or for certain teachers, may behave themselves perfectly well for you. If you face the class having already made a decision that child X will be poorly behaved, you may find that your expectations create a self-fulfilling prophecy.

GROUPING THE STUDENTS

Different schools and subject areas use a variety of different methods for grouping their students, based on their intake and also on their philosophy of education. In primary schools the children will normally be grouped by age, although sometimes (perhaps in small schools with very few children) vertical groups are created in which children of different ages work together. In the primary school, small groups of children might be pulled out of their normal classes to work in ability sets for certain subjects, or perhaps to be streamed for literacy and numeracy work.

In the secondary school, the tutor or registration groups in each year will usually contain students of mixed abilities. These mixed groups may then be put into different sets for some or all of their academic studies, perhaps starting from Year 7, or perhaps only higher up the school. In the past some schools would 'stream' their students, creating two different ability groups within a year, perhaps designated the 'A' and 'B' streams. This practice seems to be becoming less common in recent years.

It may be up to each individual head of department or faculty to decide whether to set the students: they may decide to create top, middle and bottom sets; they may use only mixed ability groups; or they could decide on a combination of both methods.

There is much discussion about whether students are better served by setting, streaming or by mixed ability teaching. You will come to your own conclusions about this, but in reality you will have little influence on the creation of groups until you gain promotion. I have based the following comments about teaching different sets and types of students purely on my own experience. They cover the advantages and disadvantages of different sets for you as a teacher, rather than from a philosophical perspective.

Teaching top sets and high ability students

- *Advantages*: It is very enjoyable to teach a group of highly motivated and intelligent children. They stretch you intellectually and there are little or no discipline problems. You will move quickly through the work and you can try out some more creative strategies. There is usually little need to differentiate the work you set.
- *Disadvantages*: Bear in mind that your marking load will be heavy, as these students are likely to work at a fast pace. You will need to be on top of your subject in order to field any awkward questions. You may also encounter ambitious parents who question the quality or quantity of your teaching. Students in top sets (or with high ability levels) can, on occasion, become arrogant or lazy because they feel that they 'know it all' already, and it is fairly difficult to decide how to discipline them for this behaviour.

Teaching mixed ability groups

- *Advantages*: There is a good mix of characters in a mixed ability group, and the stronger children may encourage the weaker ones to achieve better results. The children are generally fairly well motivated, but you will not have quite the marking load that you would have with a top set.
- *Disadvantages*: If there are disaffected children in a mixed ability group, they can affect the quality of the lesson for the more able or well motivated students. This can cause tensions within the class between those who want to learn and those who do not. You will have to differentiate the work you set if there is a wide range of abilities in the class.

Teaching bottom sets and lower ability students

- *Advantages*: If you teach a bottom set, or a group of weak students, your marking load is fairly small and you can keep well ahead of the children in terms of planning. Sometimes bottom sets are deliberately designed to contain a smaller number of students. You can use highly structured lessons and even try out some more unusual strategies that could appeal to these children. You may have support teachers or assistants to help you.

- *Disadvantages*: If the children have behavioural problems, there is the likelihood of some serious confrontations, especially if they are not willing to work hard and you are pushing them to do so. With this type of group you are not intellectually stretched by the lessons you are teaching. You may find this type of group very tiring to work with. There can be a tendency to place children with EBD in these sets as a matter of course. For those children with EBD who have high academic ability this can lead to frustrations and consequently to a worsening of behaviour.

SPECIAL EDUCATIONAL NEEDS

The special needs teachers at your school will have a great deal of expertise in this complex area, and you should always refer to them for detailed information about the types of special needs your students have, and how you can deal with them. In this section you will find some details about the more common types of special educational need, as well as some tips on how you can best access the information you need about your children, and deal with behavioural problems.

Types of special educational need

There are a huge range of different types of special need, with new conditions being recognized or named all the time. The more common types of special educational need that you are likely to come across are as follows:

- *Emotional and behavioural difficulties*: This is usually abbreviated to EBD and the term covers a wide range of problems. Students with these types of difficulties may exhibit confrontational behaviour, but equally they can be withdrawn or 'school refusers', i.e. those children who will not attend school. Bear in mind that, just because students will not behave themselves in your lessons, they do not necessarily have behavioural difficulties. Ask yourself honestly just how deep each child's problems go before you refer them to the special needs teachers. Talk to other members of staff to see whether they too have problems with an individual student.

- *Specific learning difficulties*: Again, this term is abbreviated and students are described as having a SpLD. This term also covers a wide range of problems, but the problem is only obvious in one particular area of the curriculum. An example of this would be a problem with spelling. If you see that one of your students is struggling with spelling, but is otherwise very strong academically, they could well have a specific learning difficulty.
- *Dyslexia*: This term has become very popular, with parents as well as with teachers. It is often used (wrongly) to cover a multitude of problems with spelling, writing, and so on. Do not throw this term around, using it to describe every student who ever makes a spelling mistake. If you are interested in finding out more about the subject, there is lots of information available, and new strategies for helping children with dyslexia are being developed all the time. A good starting point are the websites www.dyslexia-inst.org.uk and www.bda-dyslexia.org.uk. At the simplest level, the term describes a problem with recognizing words and this can range from mild to very severe.
- *English as a second language/English as an additional language*: These two terms, abbreviated to ESL and EAL, basically describe those students who are not fully proficient in English. They could well speak another language at home and this will probably cause them difficulties in their lessons. A student whose first language is not English might have problems with grammatical constructions and also with technical terminology.

Accessing records

It really is worth getting to know the people involved with SEN in your school as soon as possible. They can advise you on dealing with difficult students and will also fill you in on background information that helps you understand the causes of poor behaviour in your classes. They can also tell you about the specific learning needs that certain children have and how you can match your teaching content and delivery to these needs.

Ask to see the SEN records of the students you will be teaching (and tutoring) at the first possible opportunity. At the beginning of term all teachers are very busy and no one will show you these records unless you make a specific request. If you do this early on you will not have to find out about those students who have difficulties through bitter experience. You will also, hopefully, avoid saying or doing things that might exacerbate any difficult situations. Again, though, I would stress that you should not prejudge your students on this material, merely use it to inform your style of teaching and the content of your lessons.

Dealing with behavioural problems

It is sometimes the case that the child with a special educational need might become frustrated in the classroom, and consequently cause difficulties for the teacher. Alternatively, the child's need might actually be a behaviour issue. How do you deal with behavioural problems that occur with the children in your class? Look carefully at the ideas given about setting the boundaries in Chapter 3 before you start teaching. If your boundaries are clear, you will minimize poor behaviour. The case studies in the following section give detailed information on the options available to you, and the outcomes that you might expect, but here are a few brief tips for dealing with some of the more common behavioural problems:

- *Isolate the troublemaker*: Every troublemaker wants an audience: after all, a lot of misbehaviour is really attention seeking. If you isolate the child, by taking them aside and talking quietly to them rather than getting into a confrontation in front of the whole class, you are denying them the 'oxygen of publicity'.
- *Get down to their level*: It is much easier to reason with someone if you are *literally* on the same level as them. If the student is seated, crouch down beside the child to chat. This immediately makes you seem more reasonable and lessens the authoritarian image that some teachers have which can lead to confrontations.
- *Remain reasonable at all times*: It is very hard to be angry with someone who refuses to rise to the bait. If you remain calm and reasonable at all times, this should have a direct impact on a rude or confrontational student. Again, the child will not receive the attention he or she is seeking. Perhaps, at home, the only way for such children to get a reaction from their parents or guardians is to become confrontational. The reaction they expect from you is probably for you to shout and get angry. If you refuse to do this, you will defuse the situation and start to train the student to trust you.

- *Keep your voice quiet*: If you can, learn to keep your voice low and quiet; this will help calm the situation down and force the child to slow down and consider the behaviour in a clearer way. Put yourself in the child's shoes and think about the difference between someone shouting back at you when you are angry, or staying calm. This tip will also stop you from becoming a loud teacher and possibly wearing out your voice.
- *Explain the problem*: Often, a child simply will not understand why or what they are doing wrong. Explain why the behaviour is inappropriate, ask the child if he or she agrees with you and understands what you are saying. By doing this, you are giving the student a chance to address and change antisocial or inappropriate behaviour.
- *Stick to your guns*: Back to those boundaries again! You are the teacher, you have set the rules and been fair and clear about it. Do not give in to pacify a child. If you do, you are storing up trouble for yourself in the future.
- *State the sanction clearly*: Staying calm and reasonable, inform the child of what will happen if the misbehaviour continues. If the student (and the class) see that you stick to your boundaries at all times, they will know the outcome of any misbehaviour.
- *Depersonalize the sanction*: Instead of making the child feel that he or she is receiving a personal reprimand, try to depersonalize the punishment you are going to give by saying: '*If you continue to [state misbehaviour] I will have no option but to [state sanction].*' This helps to make you seem reasonable and fair.

CASE STUDIES

The following case studies are fictitious and reflect a variety of the situations you may have to face. The case studies give details about the student, what the problem is, and offer some ideas about how the teacher could deal with this. These are only examples, and much of how you deal with real-life problems depends on the situation you find yourself in, the type of class you have and the child's reactions to what you do and say. However, the case studies should provide a useful starting point from which to work during your NQT year.

The 'odd one out'

The student

Joe is rather a strange child. He lacks social skills and does not integrate well with the rest of the class. If you are honest, you can understand why they do not want to work with him. His behaviour is strange and he can become quite confrontational if the other children do not accept his ideas.

At the start of term, the students were willing to work with Joe, but as time goes on they are becoming increasingly frustrated by him and keep asking you not to make them work with him. You are becoming worried about what might happen if someone refuses point blank to co-operate.

Dealing with the problem

1. The first step to take is to find out, if you have not already, whether Joe is on the SEN list. If he is, you should ask for some more information about exactly what his problem is and what has caused it. If he is not officially recognized as having special needs, bring his problems to the attention of the appropriate person. He clearly has some sort of emotional or behavioural difficulty, in the form of a problem socializing, and this needs to be addressed as soon as possible.
2. It certainly might be worthwhile taking Joe to one side, perhaps after your lesson, and discussing with him why he has trouble relating to the other children. You will need to be subtle about this, perhaps asking him if he feels he is settling in okay and if not, why not. You could also offer him some strategies to help him get on with the other students better, for instance, listening carefully to other people's ideas.
3. At the start of the term you will, hopefully, have set the boundaries (see Chapter 3) and *all* the students must follow them. If any children refuse to work with Joe, simply state to them that they must respect the others in the class by working in the group you have put them in. Follow the appropriate sanctions if they refuse to do so.
4. Another option is to 'fix' the groups to avoid any difficult combinations (see 'Creating groups' in Chapter 3, p. 53). This

avoids the possibility of confrontation, but these children (although they do not realize it) are influencing your teaching and you are not really addressing the root of the problem.
5. If appropriate to your subject, or if you teach Joe PSE, you could do some work on making friends with the whole class in the hope that Joe will pick up some tips.

The potentially violent student

The student

Thelma is well known around the school for her violent temper, which seems to flare up out of the blue. She is usually a fairly well motivated student and she has produced some good work for you. However, she does have a tendency to argue with a couple of the other children in your class.

At the moment these arguments are only verbal, but they are getting increasingly vicious and you worry that they may flare up into physical violence. You can sense a lot of tension building up within the class.

Dealing with the problem

1. Again, the first step is to check whether the SEN department knows that Thelma has a behavioural difficulty. If not, bring her to their attention. Ask for their advice on how you should deal with Thelma, as they may know about specific events or actions that make her temper flare up.
2. Talk to Thelma individually about her behaviour, and try to help her work out what it is that makes her angry and how she might deal with it in an appropriate way. This may prove difficult if she also gets confrontational with you. Try to explain to her how other students and teachers feel about her behaviour rather than blaming her. Teach Thelma some relaxation and anger management techniques, for instance, counting down from 10 when she feels herself getting upset with someone.
3. Sit Thelma as far away as possible from those children with whom she becomes confrontational. If possible, sit her next to

a well behaved but placid student in your class. However, make sure that this child does not suffer because Thelma is sitting next to him or her. Another alternative would be to sit her at the front of the classroom so that she cannot see or talk to any other students. If she becomes confrontational when asked to do this, explain to her that you are trying to help her control her temper by avoiding situations where it becomes a problem.

4. If Thelma does get into a confrontation, always try to defuse the situation by talking to her quietly, moving her away from the person she is quarrelling with, or by asking her to step outside to calm down (perhaps with a friend). If a violent confrontation seems likely to take place, remove Thelma from the classroom as quickly as possible. You might want to offer Thelma the option of going to sit in a quiet and private area as soon as she feels herself about to blow.

The student with poor concentration

The student

Fred generally behaves well in class, but he has a problem with finishing his work. His confidence in his work is very low and he rarely concentrates long enough to complete anything. He complains of tiredness if you ask him to write for more than five minutes at a time.

Fred's work is often very difficult to read and he has now started to distract other students near him by chatting to them when he runs out of steam. He very rarely completes his homework.

Dealing with the problem

1. Again, talk to the SEN department. It may be that Fred has a genuine problem concentrating because of a specific learning difficulty. This might also explain the poor presentation of his work – perhaps he is hiding the fact that he cannot spell or perhaps he does not understand the work you are doing.
2. Give him small but achievable targets when you are doing written work. For instance, put a line half-way down the page

and ask him to aim to write down to that point by the end of the time given. Alternatively, you could ask him to aim to write as neatly as possible, rather than trying to complete the work.

3. Talk to him about why it is important for him to work neatly and complete the tasks you set. Ask him if there is a problem that you can help him with. At the same time, though, you must stick to the boundaries you have set for the class and sanction him for uncompleted homework and for chatting in lessons. Hopefully this will encourage him to concentrate.

4. It is possibly worth phoning Fred's parents or guardians to talk to them about his homework. This can often help a great deal by identifying the problem for them and showing the child that you care. They could spend time with him at home to help him complete his work.

5. He may find it helpful to work on a computer, as it is possibly the act of writing that is tiring him. If your school has a portable computer, you could ask to use it. Alternatively, you could use trips for the class to the computer room as a reward to encourage Fred. Another possibility for Fred might be tape recording some of his written work, rather than writing it.

The arrogant student

The student

Sandra is a very self-confident student, but her confidence often comes across as arrogance. She completes all the work you set to a high standard, but she has started taking liberties with her behaviour in your lessons, talking while you are explaining the work and so on.

Sandra has started arriving late for class. When you ask her where she has been, she always has some sort of excuse, but never has a note to prove it. You believe she is lying to you. Whenever you try to challenge her about her behaviour, she says your lessons are boring and she doesn't enjoy them. She frequently says (loudly) that Mr Evans, the teacher they had last year, was much better than you. She also asks you repeatedly if you are a new teacher and others in the class are picking up on this.

Dealing with the problem

This type of student can be surprisingly hard to deal with, as they do not have a special educational need but they can really disrupt your class without actually earning any sanctions. They can also severely undermine your self-confidence, especially if you are an inexperienced teacher.

1. Stick rigidly to your boundaries and if Sandra does overstep the mark, apply the appropriate sanction. For instance, explain to her that being late without a note means that she will receive a punishment that you will impose on her just as you would on any other member of the class. Make sure that you are fair and that she receives the same treatment as everyone else. That way, she cannot complain.

2. It is very tempting, when a student says your lessons are boring, to respond in a negative way. You may not feel particularly confident about what you are teaching and this type of comment can be very hurtful. Fight against the temptation to throw a jibe back at Sandra: this is exactly what this type of student usually wants – attention. If she knows she is succeeding in hurting you then she will continue to do so. The best response (apart from ignoring her) is a bored, 'Really, that's interesting.'

3. It is possibly worth talking to her about her behaviour and explaining why you feel it is unacceptable. Be aware, though, that in doing this you are acknowledging that she is getting to you. If she feels she has succeeded this may be just what she needs to step up her campaign. You could ask a more senior or experienced teacher to have a word with her, but again you run the risk of undermining your authority.

4. Overall, the best response is to completely blank her any time she says or does anything designed to attract your attention. If you get into a slanging match, she has won.

The unhappy or shy student

The student

Selina is a quiet, well behaved child. She rarely puts her hand up in class, but she always completes her work quickly and neatly. In fact, the other students call her a 'boffin'. You have also heard them laughing at her glasses.

She doesn't seem to have any friends in your class and you often see her wandering alone around the school at break and lunch-time. Recently she has become even more withdrawn in lessons.

Dealing with the problem

1. It seems possible, from the information here, that Selina is being bullied. In the secondary school, the first approach is to talk or write a note to her form tutor, rather than speaking directly to Selina, to see whether this is a possibility. In the primary school, keep an eye out to see whether there are low-level incidents of bullying taking place in your classroom. You might also ask a playtime supervisor whether anyone has been spotted bullying Selina.

2. If you have built a strong relationship with Selina, then you could ask her what is wrong. Perhaps she came from a different school or area to all the other children and does not know anybody. You could mention that you have noticed that she is very quiet in class and ask her whether she wants to talk to you about anything. However, you do want to avoid making her feel even worse.

3. Try every way you can to improve Selina's self-confidence. Praise her work, preferably in written comments rather than in front of the class, to avoid the others developing this idea of her as a 'boffin'. You could also try to encourage her to become more of a participant in class discussions, but be wary of forcing her to answer questions.

4. Again, you could phone her parents or guardians, after consulting the appropriate pastoral manager. They might not realize that Selina is finding school so hard. It is probably best not to tell her that you have telephoned home, as this could make her feel even worse.

5. Try to encourage other children, perhaps ones you know are sensitive, to see if they can include her in break and lunch-time activities. You could also suggest that Selina joins a homework club or other activity that takes place during breaks, so she has somewhere to go and also so that she has the opportunity to make friends.

6. In the secondary school, ask her form tutor whether she has any friends in her form group. If she does, it could be worth putting her in the same class as these students for your subject, even if this means moving her to a different group.

The verbally aggressive student

The student

Colin is an extremely difficult student and the SEN department have told you that he has severe emotional and behavioural difficulties. He claims that you pick on him and whenever you try to tell him off or ask him to complete work he reacts badly, throwing abuse at you. The standard of his written work is very poor and he rarely finishes anything.

Colin is also confrontational with the other children and none of them want to work with him. Your class has quite a few difficult children in it and you feel that Colin is dragging them down with him.

Dealing with the problem

1. Ask a special needs teacher to talk to you about Colin. If possible, try to find out the background to his problems so that you can avoid exacerbating the situation: perhaps it is something specific that sets him off. Ask for advice about how to deal with him and consider requesting a support teacher for your lessons.
2. Be as fair and firm as you can, sticking closely to the boundaries you have set and explaining why his behaviour warrants the sanction you give. Make it clear that, rather than the sanction being your choice, it is his choice because of the way he is behaving. At times you may need to bend your boundaries a little with this type of student, depending on how severe the problem is. You do not want to have to send the student out of every lesson, but they must understand that you will stick to your guns.
3. Use praise as much as you can – whenever you see Colin doing something even slightly well, commend him for it. It is very

easy to slip into negative behaviour with a child like this, as you get very frustrated and the way that they treat you can be hurtful. Always keep in mind that this child has special problems and must have a very difficult life to behave like this: do not take what they say and do personally.

4. Try to get Colin working with some very good students, who will not respond to any disruptive behaviour and who will hopefully motivate him. Use careful praise of these children to encourage him to emulate them. Offer some really good rewards to the whole class and try to ensure that Colin wins one of them.

5. Again, it is probably worth telephoning or meeting the parents or guardians (perhaps before the parents' evening, if it is not early on in the year). A chat with them could shed light on why he behaves as he does, but do be careful about what you say.

Chapter 9

Staff

Teaching attracts a diverse range of people, some of whom will have started on their careers many years ago and will have years of experience, others who may be young NQTs just starting out in the profession. A large secondary school may have as many as 100 teachers, working in various different departments. There will also be a huge number of other staff: from catering to cleaning workers, from science technicians to office staff. Even in a small primary school there will be a whole range of teaching and non-teaching staff working together as part of the team responsible for running the school.

In this chapter you can find lots of tips and ideas about working with other members of staff at your school. This includes information about who you should get to know, as well as some light-hearted details of different 'types' of teachers, and some ideas about working with support staff, and with senior management.

GETTING TO KNOW THE RIGHT PEOPLE

Teachers (and other school staff) are, on the whole, incredibly good at supporting and helping each other. Make it a priority, early on in your induction year, to get to know the people who can help make your working life much easier. Some examples are given below:

- *The union reps*: If you belong to a union, or are thinking of joining one, it really is worth getting to know any union representatives in your school as they can answer a variety of questions you may have. If it should ever be necessary for you to have a meeting with senior management, the union representative can come along to this to act as a mediator or advisor and to ensure that you are treated fairly.

- *Heads of department*: It is also well worth being on speaking terms with the heads of the various departments in a secondary school. If you decide to do any cross-curricular work, these teachers are a source of very useful information.
- *Curriculum co-ordinators*: Similarly, in the primary school there should be curriculum co-ordinators who are responsible for overseeing the various areas of the curriculum. These teachers will generally be subject specialists in their particular area, and will have a good bank of knowledge, ideas and teaching materials that you can utilize with your own class.
- *Experienced teachers*: In some schools you will find a layer of experienced teachers who have not gone for promotion to a more senior level, but who prefer to stay within the classroom. It is very helpful for you to get to know these people – to find someone you feel you could talk to if you have a query that may seem petty, but which is really worrying you.
- *Your induction tutor*: You will of course need to get to know your induction tutor right at the start of term. The type of relationship you develop will depend on who has been appointed in this role. If your tutor is a senior member of staff, he or she is likely to be busy and you may have to chase for time to meet up and talk.
- *Office staff*: Teachers sometimes overlook the office staff in a school, perhaps because they do not normally have much contact with them, and this is a shame. Office staff can make your life a lot easier, for instance, if you have a letter you need typing, or if you need information about a student, such as telephone numbers, addresses, etc. Take the time to get to know them; they perform a very valuable role in the running of the school and will generally be very happy to help you. If the headteacher has a secretary, try to get to know him or her as well. If you need fast access to the head or approval for something, for instance, a trip, an amenable head's secretary can smooth your path.
- *Buildings staff*: Another important group of people involved in the running of the school, who again are often overlooked, are the buildings or caretaking staff. These might include a buildings

manager, caretaker, cleaners, and so on. Again, it is very worthwhile being on speaking terms with these people. If, for instance, you need to book the hall or have some chairs moved at short notice, a good relationship with the buildings staff will smooth your way. The job of cleaning a school is a very difficult one, so think about how you might help the cleaners with their task. For instance, it might be helpful for your classes to put the chairs on the tables at the end of the day. You will certainly be assisting the cleaners if you ensure that your classroom floor is kept as clear of rubbish as possible.

- *Special educational needs staff*: Finally, do get to know the teachers involved with special educational needs in your school. If you show an interest, they will have lots of valuable advice that they can give you about handling your more difficult students and they can probably offer you some more specialized resources for your classes. You will also find it easier to gain access to student records if you are on speaking terms with these teachers. Again, their role is a crucial one in the smooth running of the school, and one that is perhaps underestimated at times.

GETTING TO KNOW THE WRONG PEOPLE

Unfortunately, there may also be some people in your school who you should avoid like the plague. These are the people who have stayed in teaching because they cannot (or cannot be bothered to) get another job. To them, teaching is not a vocation but an irritation. They will moan at every opportunity (and to anyone who will listen) about how dreadful the students are. Teaching is, of course, a tough job, and I would never try to deny that fact. However, the only way to give the students a fair deal (and to enjoy the job) is to work hard at it. Try as far as you can to avoid getting involved with this type of teacher, whose cynicism and jaded attitude could quickly wear you down.

TYPES OF TEACHERS

Here are some examples of types of teachers you may encounter and details about the way they might behave, inside and outside the classroom. These examples are entirely fictitious. I have made them rather stereotypical and, hopefully, amusing. Teachers are individuals and use a mixture of styles in the classroom, depending as much on the class as on their own personality. However, you might like to see if you can recognize any of these teachers in your own school or even if you recognize any of the qualities listed in yourself.

The 'old-school-tie' teacher

- *Dress code*: This type of teacher always dresses smartly and, if male, wears a suit and tie. They feel school uniform is vital for maintaining discipline amongst the children.
- *Favourite catchphrases*: The 'old-school-tie' teacher often uses sentences starting with *'In my day ...'*, for instance, *'In my day children knew how to behave themselves.'* He or she also uses the question, *'Would you do that at home?'* for various misdemeanours, for instance, if a child puts his or her feet up on a desk.
- *Discipline code*: This teacher is a strict disciplinarian who believes that children or pupils (never students) should be seen and not heard.
- *Favourite method of discipline*: This type of teacher would like to use the cane, but since they cannot, they will give their children a verbal thrashing instead. They are keen on giving out vast quantities of lines and lots of detentions. They also like to send children to stand outside the classroom, where they immediately forget about them until the inspectors or the headteacher arrive, at which point they instantly become a model teacher.
- *Teaching style*: There is a strong focus on traditional methods and working in silence in this teacher's lessons. There will be little exploratory or creative work.
- *Marking strategy*: This type of teacher uses a red pen to put lots of crosses, a few ticks, and a mark out of ten on each piece of work.
- *Bad habits*: The 'old-school-tie' teacher has a tendency to turn red and spit when he or she gets angry, which is rather frequently. The male of the species has a poor taste in ties. Irritatingly for you, they like moaning out loud (but not to anyone in particular) in the staff room.
- *Classroom layout*: The desks are invariably in rows, facing the teacher.
- *Condition of desk*: Their own desk will be very neat, with only one pile of marking to be done and lots of red pens to use when

doing it. Do not, whatever you do, borrow a pen or move any of their papers.

- *Advantages*: The children will know where they stand with this type of teacher and will probably be well disciplined, although unfortunately this is often through fear rather than respect. He or she will usually achieve good results with able, well motivated children.
- *Disadvantages*: Quiet children are often too scared to answer questions in this teacher's lessons and there is little opportunity for group work. Weaker children may exhibit bad behaviour as an excuse to escape from the classroom.
- *Marks/10*:
  Educational value = 7
  Development of creativity and imagination = 2
  Quality of discipline = 7
  Equality of opportunity = 2
  Scale of student appreciation = 2
- *Total score/50*: 20

'The students are my mates' teacher

- *Dress code*: This teacher dresses in a casual style, often wearing trendy labels. He or she tries to dress like the students to get 'in' with them. They are not keen on the idea of school uniform and tend to overlook minor infringements of the rules.
- *Favourite catchphrases*: Again, this teacher tries to emulate the students: '*Check it out*' is a current favourite. If a fight between two students starts, they will try, '*C'mon, let's be reasonable about this, guys.*'
- *Discipline code*: They base their discipline code on the theory that, if you let the students do what they want, they are likely to work harder. This type of teacher feels comfortable with lots of noise and activity.
- *Favourite method of discipline*: He or she believes that: '*The students will discipline themselves if they feel sufficiently motivated and any misdemeanours are an expression of the students' frustration at an outmoded schooling system, which denies young people a sense of identity and seeks to destroy their natural creativity.*'
- *Teaching style*: There will be lots of exploration and issues-based

work, usually in groups. This teacher avoids traditional methods such as 'chalk and talk'.

- *Marking strategy*: This teacher only gives positive comments and feels that using red ink will demotivate the students. They are also strongly against the concept of a right or wrong answer, even in fact-based subjects.
- *Bad habits*: Among this teacher's bad habits are: talking while the class are chatting; using too much jargon when talking to other teachers; and drinking alcohol and smoking (sometimes *with* the students!).
- *Classroom layout*: Desks are usually set out in groups, but sometimes he or she likes to get rid of the furniture altogether and have an impromptu 'drama session'. There will generally be much movement of desks, often in *your* classroom. They are unlikely to return the furniture to its original position.
- *State of desk*: Their desk is neat, but only because all their papers are in one pile. At the bottom of the pile is that really urgent report that this teacher should have completed three weeks ago.
- *Advantages*: The students will probably like this type of teacher, partly because they will feel relaxed, but also because they will be able to get away with murder. This teaching style encourages creativity and individuality.
- *Disadvantages*: Unless the students have a natural sense of discipline, chaos will probably reign. The class will be very noisy and this may trouble students who would prefer to concentrate on their work.
- *Marks/10*:
  Educational value = 7
  Development of creativity and imagination = 10
  Quality of discipline = 3
  Equality of opportunity = 6
  Scale of student appreciation = 7
- *Total score/50*:   33

The ultra-efficient teacher

- *Dress code*: The ultra-efficient teacher always dresses smartly: if male he wears a suit and tie, if female she wears a smart jacket, often with a skirt. He or she feels that school uniform is important and will impose the school rules on a fair and consistent basis.

- *Favourite catchphrases*: 'I'd like you all to face the front, make eye contact and listen carefully.'
- *Discipline code*: The ultra-efficient teacher has a strong sense of discipline, but is not necessarily seen as strict by the children. This type of teacher believes that everyone has an equal right to a good education and will impose the discipline necessary to achieve this.
- *Favourite method of discipline*: He or she will apply any school behaviour code to the letter and will contact the home if they feel a child is consistently misbehaving.
- *Teaching style*: The lessons will be very clear and well organized with a good balance between teacher- and student-led sessions.
- *Marking strategy*: This teacher combines written comments on the work with close marking of errors.
- *Bad habits*: This teacher's bad habits include a refusal to see the worst in any child and a tendency to cosy up to senior management because of their ambition to get promotion quickly. Irritatingly for mere mortals, their reports are always beautifully presented and handed in on time, or even before the deadline.
- *Classroom layout*: The desks are usually set out in rows, facing the teacher, but the ultra-efficient teacher sometimes moves the furniture for group work and will always return it to its previous position.
- *State of desk*: Their own desk is neat, with lesson plans for each day carefully laid out in advance. Photocopied resources for the next three weeks will be ready for use.
- *Advantages*: The children know where they stand and will respond well to a teacher who applies consistent standards. Their work will be neatly presented and all children will be given equality of opportunity.
- *Disadvantages*: Creativity is sometimes stifled, but this is not always the case. This type of teacher can be rather depressing for other staff, as they feel that they could never be so efficient.
- *Marks/10*:
  Educational value = 9
  Development of creativity and imagination = 7
  Quality of discipline = 9
  Equality of opportunity = 9
  Scale of student appreciation = 7
- *Total score/50*: 41

The joker

- *Dress code*: The joker wears fairly casual, usually 'fun' clothes, for instance, brightly coloured ties and T-shirts with amusing captions on them. They couldn't care less about school uniform.
- *Favourite catchphrases*: The joker starts most lessons by saying: '*Do you want to hear a joke?*' In fact, this is their favourite question to the students and to the staff. The joke will invariably be rude.
- *Discipline code*: This type of teacher feels that if the students find the lessons funny, they will behave themselves. Surprisingly, this actually often works.
- *Favourite method of discipline*: The joker disciplines classes by making fun of any student who misbehaves. Joke punishments include the student standing in the corner, on one leg, hands on head.
- *Teaching style*: This teacher uses lots of anecdotes from his or her life to illustrate the subject being taught. For instance, geography work on polluted rivers may consist of a story about the time the joker and his or her mates got drunk and threw a shopping trolley into the local river. A lot of lesson time is spent with the students listening to the teacher talking and telling jokes, during which he or she likes to jump up on the desks to add variety.
- *Marking strategy*: The students' books will be full of jokey comments that he or she is perfectly happy for them to respond to.
- *Bad habits*: See 'favourite catchphrases' (telling bad jokes) and 'dress code' (wearing bad ties). The joker also tends to get rather strange haircuts.
- *Classroom layout*: The desks are set out in rows, facing the teacher, not because of any particular educational philosophy, but so that all the students can hear the jokes properly and see any accompanying demonstrations.
- *State of desk*: The joker is not renowned for his or her tidiness. They will probably have a drawer full of handy practical jokes to play on teachers and students.
- *Advantages*: The students tend to respond well to this type of teacher. A lot of school can be very boring, so it's good for them to have a laugh. They will also (hopefully) respect the joker.
- *Disadvantages*: Not a lot of subject teaching goes on because the

joker spends so much time telling his or her jokes. The quiet students tend to just sit there while the louder ones will join in and probably get more attention.

- *Marks/10*:
Educational value = 6
Development of creativity and imagination = 9
Quality of discipline = 7
Equality of opportunity = 6
Scale of student appreciation = 9
- *Total score/50*: 37

The chaos theory teacher

- *Dress code*: This type of teacher looks as if their outfit was thrown together in a force ten hurricane in about ten seconds that morning. Their hair looks slept on and has not seen a comb in recent history.
- *Favourite catchphrases*: This teacher is usually spotted wandering around the staffroom asking, '*Has anybody got a red pen I can borrow?*' As exam time draws near, this will change to: '*I'm sure I had that set of really important GCSE exam papers a minute ago ... now where did I put them?*'
- *Discipline code*: What discipline code? Chaos rules here and the students must sink or swim. Some of the students are quite happy sitting at the back of the room on the floor smoking a cigarette.
- *Favourite method of discipline*: This type of teacher believes that having a chat to the offenders to try and discover what makes them tick will work miracles.
- *Teaching style*: The chaos theory teacher practises what is known as 'discovery learning'. This translates as 'the kids do what they like and hopefully a little bit of learning takes place, probably incidentally'. He or she may be a real expert on their subject, but can have trouble putting the information across.
- *Marking strategy*: Their marking strategy is straightforward and works every time: just lose the books before you have to mark them.
- *Bad habits*: Disgustingly, this teacher has a habit of absent-mindedly picking their nose or scratching their bottom. For other bad habits see also 'marking strategy' (losing books) and 'dress code' (incredibly messy).

- *Classroom layout*: The desks are usually set out in rows, to impose a little bit of order on the class. However, by the end of the lesson the rows are disbanded altogether (by the students, rather than by the teacher) and the desks positioned so that friends can sit together.
- *State of desk*: Their desk looks as if the proverbial bomb has hit it. This is in fact probably one of the main reasons for this teacher's marking strategy: somewhere beneath the debris are those vital exam papers and all those lost exercise books!
- *Advantages*: They are usually a real expert on their subject and the students will respond well to this. Their teaching style can also lead to some very creative ideas.
- *Disadvantages*: The bright kids may do well, but the less able tend to get lost in the whirlwind that this teacher lives in.
- *Marks/10*:
  Educational value = 7
  Development of creativity and imagination = 8
  Quality of discipline = 2
  Equality of opportunity = 4
  Scale of student appreciation = 7
- *Total score/50*:   29

The earth mother or father

- *Dress code*: If female, this teacher wears a long pinafore dress, sometimes made of corduroy, and flat shoes with her hair tied back in a bun. If male, you can spot him by his 'Jesus' sandals (worn, in impeccable style, with socks) and his long beard.
- *Favourite catchphrases*: *'Now then, children, let's all settle down and do some work, shall we?'* is used by this teacher as the class start to riot. Students are called 'children' by the earth mother or father up to the age of about 15.
- *Discipline code*: This type of teacher tries to encourage self-discipline in his or her children, as they feel that it is wrong for teachers to be too disciplinarian. He or she asks quietly for silence and is usually noisily ignored.
- *Favourite method of discipline*: The earth mother or father believes in talking to the children about why they did what they did and why they shouldn't do it again.
- *Teaching style*: Their style is soft and gently spoken. The lessons

tend to consist of talking to the class for a while then asking them to explore a topic. This teacher rarely raises his or her voice, except when they begin to panic as they realize the class is rioting and the head is coming down the corridor.

- *Marking strategy*: In a nutshell, this teacher's marking strategy involves positive comments only, and no red pen or crosses allowed.
- *Bad habits*: His or her bad habits include talking while the children are talking; not washing their hair very frequently; and wearing socks with sandals.
- *Classroom layout*: The desks are set out in groups, so that the children can 'share their ideas'. There are lots of environmentally friendly posters on the walls.
- *State of desk*: The earth mother or father has a neat desk, with lots of little personal items, such as a cuddly toy, a photo of his or her family, and so on.
- *Advantages*: This type of teacher is usually good for quiet and weak children, as they will receive lots of personal attention and a gentle, caring approach.
- *Disadvantages*: There may be poor classroom control; the lessons do not stretch the more able; and those with behavioural difficulties may take advantage.
- *Marks/10*:
  Educational value = 7
  Development of creativity and imagination = 7
  Quality of discipline = 6
  Equality of opportunity = 6
  Scale of student appreciation = 7
- *Total score/50*:   33

WORKING WITH SUPPORT STAFF

If you are lucky enough to have support staff working with you, the help and expertise on offer can be a very valuable asset in your NQT year and beyond. The type of support staff you might encounter will include classroom assistants, special needs workers, learning support assistants, and so on. Take some time early on in the school year to sit down with any support staff you have, and start to develop a good working relationship. Often, a support teacher will have prior experience with a particular class or student on which you can draw. Your assistant might have some excellent ideas that could prove invaluable in developing your own teaching practice. Find out how your assistant prefers to work – would he or she like to be involved in lesson planning, in differentiating certain tasks, or in simply delivering the work that you prepare? Does the assistant prefer to work within the classroom setting, or to take individuals or small groups to work elsewhere?

DEALING WITH SENIOR MANAGEMENT

In your first year it is likely that you will have very little reason to deal directly with senior management. The first person you turn to when you have problems will usually be your induction tutor, your line manager or, in a secondary school, the head of your department, or a head of year or other pastoral manager (if the problems are with your registration group). If you choose to apply for promotion, you will have increasing contact with senior managers as you progress, but at this stage in your career you will not usually have any reason to approach them.

It is always worth having senior members of staff on your side, as they can assist you if you have any major problems or if you need approval, for instance, of a trip or of time off. Members of the senior management of a school are 'on duty' at all times, so remember this when you are dealing with them. Be careful what you say – you may believe that you are making a joke, but they might take what you see as humorous comments in the wrong way. Finally, bear in mind just who it is that decides promotions in a school.

Chapter 10

Parents

This chapter deals with the aspects of your job where you will be working with, and reporting to, the children's parents or guardians. Here you will find ideas about developing your relationship with parents, thoughts about coping with the parents' evening, and also an examination of some of the different types of parents you might meet. I use the term 'parents' throughout this chapter to describe whoever takes care of the child at home. There are many different types of family unit and a wide range of people who will be responsible for caring for your students. The term 'parents' is used to include all of these: from single parent families, to guardians such as foster parents, grandparents, brothers and sisters and so on.

DEVELOPING THE TEACHER–PARENT RELATIONSHIP

If you use the analogy between a school and a business, the parents of a student are the clients of the business. Of course, unless you are working at a private school, the parents will not be paying directly for your 'services', but indirectly, through taxation. However, they are still entitled to know (and will demand) that the service offered by your school, and by you individually as a teacher, matches their expectations. As in any business, it is important to develop a good relationship with the people with whom you are working. This is especially important in education, of course, because the parents can back up the work that you do in school with their children at home. Here are some ideas about how you might develop your own relationship with the parents of your children:

- *Explain how they can support you*: Many parents would like to support the work that teachers do in the school, but are unsure of how they might go about doing this. Take the time to communicate this information to them. Perhaps they can help by doing 20 minutes reading with their children each night, maybe you would welcome some parental support with learning spellings, or with keeping tabs on behaviour.
- *Use them as a source of information*: Another idea is to ask your children to bring in information gathered at home from their family, for instance, details of a family tree for a history project or statistics about the size of the family for mathematics work. You could also ask your students to tape a conversation with their parents, perhaps for use in a project about the local area or about where the different students come from.
- *Invite them into your classroom/school*: Some parents are willing to help to the extent that they will actually come into the classroom to assist the teacher. If this would be useful to you, then do find out whether any of your parents would be interested. They might help with listening to readers or supervising the putting up of displays. Alternatively, some parents are very keen to help with more general school events, such as the parent who would sew some costumes for the school play.
- *Get involved with your PTA*: Schools will usually have a parent-teacher group, the Parent-Teacher Association (PTA), that aims to strengthen the links between home and school. This group will also have a role in raising funds for the school. If you have the time or inclination, it can be useful to become involved with the PTA. You may also find that you want to request some of the funds they raise for a project in your own class or department.

COMMUNICATING WITH PARENTS

When we are looking to develop a strong relationship with the parents of the children we teach, it is vital to keep the channels of communication open. There are a whole range of different ways in which teachers communicate with parents:

- *The informal chat*: If you teach in a primary school, you will probably meet most of the parents of your students on a daily basis: in the morning when they drop the child off at school, and in the afternoon when they pick them up. It will be fairly straightforward to develop some sort of relationship and communicate any worries. If you do need to talk to a parent in more detail, it is usually not too difficult to request a quick meeting after school.

- *The formal report*: One of the main formalized communications with the home is through any formal reports during the school year. Reports offer a good form of communication, although they have their limitations. The report is often a rather one-way process, the teacher informing the parents rather than having a dialogue with them. In some schools, the parents or students are asked to give a response to the report and this is a useful step towards building a dialogue.
- *The parents' evening*: The parents' evening offers a better chance to communicate with parents, although again this is only a brief encounter and in reality offers little opportunity for extensive conversation. You can find lots more information below about parents' evenings.
- *The telephone call*: One of the best ways to communicate with parents is by telephoning them, because it is such a direct and instant method. When considering using the telephone, don't always focus on calling about negative incidents – an excellent way to motivate your children is to promise a call home for a more positive reason. For instance, you might phone about an incident of particularly good behaviour; or to report excellent progress on some targets set. Before you call home, do check with the appropriate manager that it is acceptable. Telephoning parents is especially effective if a student is not completing homework, or has missed time at school without a valid reason (this, of course, comes under the role of the form tutor). You should be able to find the relevant telephone number in the register or by asking the office staff for assistance. If you talk directly to a parent in this way, you will usually find them more than willing to back you up. The students also seem remarkably impressed by the fact that you have phoned home – I would suggest this is partly because you have taken an interest, and partly because most students genuinely care about what their parents think of them.

- *The letter*: Most schools (and many secondary departments) will have a variety of standard letters that you can send home, for instance, if coursework is missing or if a child is absent without reason. This will save you the time spent in making a telephone call, particularly if you have difficulty getting through. However, sending a letter does lack the directness of speaking to a parent on the phone.

THE PARENTS' EVENING

One of the scariest experiences in your induction year will be your first ever parents' evening. As a student teacher, although you may have come into contact with parents or guardians, you will not have had to face them in such a formalized setting. Here are a few thoughts that may help you prepare for the nerve-racking occasion that is the parents' evening. Do bear in mind that after a few of these experiences you will wonder what you were ever scared about.

Appointments

In the run-up to the parents' evening you may be asked to book time slots for each parent or guardian. Do not worry too much about the accuracy of this. Inevitably, people are late or get delayed talking to other teachers and it is rare that you will actually stick to the appointment times. These appointment times do, however, help to give the students a sense that the parents' evening is an important event for them.

If you do not have many students, try to bunch the appointments together so that you don't have to wait for long periods of time. You could, if you wish, leave yourself free for the first half hour so that you have longer to relax after school. On the other hand you may have a large number of classes (for instance, if you teach a subject such as music or drama where you only see the students for one lesson a week). If this is the case I would recommend that you ask only those students about whom you have concerns to make an appointment. The others, if they really want to see you, should of course be given the opportunity.

Preparation

Do not try to make copious amounts of notes before the parents' evening. It is unlikely you will refer to them – it is better to be natural and talk to the parents or guardians about your own impressions of their child. If you feel it would help, have a few points written down that you would like to raise with them, perhaps a concern about homework, or a query about an extended period of absence.

Try to give yourself a break before the evening starts. You may find that there is half an hour to an hour between the end of school and the start of the parents' evening. Make sure you have something to eat, as you may not finish until late. It is also a good idea to change your clothes, because you can bring a 'smart' outfit with you and also because you may feel rather 'creased' after a day's teaching. Looking business-like will help you feel ready to face the parents.

They're more scared of you ...

As with the first time your students meet you (see Chapter 1) you will find that some of the parents or guardians are more scared of you than you are of them. Keep this in mind and try to put them at ease. This will help you relax too. When they arrive, stand up and shake hands with them and identify which student they 'belong' to. If the child is with them, you have an added advantage, as you can praise (or embarrass) the student in front of his or her parents. If the student is there, a good starter question is: '*How do you think you've been getting on?*'

The discussion

Keep your discussion short and concise. There is no need to waffle on, as it will make you tired and will have little value. Comment on the student's work to date and give some ideas for targets that the parents or guardians may be able to help with, for example, ensuring homework is completed properly. If they have any specific queries that you are not sure about, make a brief note and say that you will talk to your head of department or a more senior teacher. Do ask the parents if they have any questions. They may well feel scared to ask you and this is also a good way of bringing the interview to an end.

Problems/problem parents

Although it is very unusual, you may find yourself in a situation where the parents or guardians become confrontational with you, perhaps criticizing the way you teach or the type of work you are setting. As an inexperienced teacher, this can be very difficult to deal with. If this does happen, try to remain calm and rational, using the techniques discussed in Chapter 3 to defuse the situation. You could suggest arranging a meeting between you, the parents and your head of department at another time. In this way they can discuss their concerns in private and you will have the support of a more senior, experienced colleague to help you deal with them.

Missing

Inevitably, some parents or guardians will not turn up, either because they could not make it, or because they did not want to come (or because the student did not tell them that there was a parents' evening). In fact, it is often the case that the parents you most want or need to talk to do not turn up. Do try to check up on any students you are worried about. Your school may have a system whereby they do this for you, but if you do have strong concerns make a phone call home yourself (having told the appopriate pastoral manager that you are going to do so).

TYPES OF PARENT

You will come across a variety of parents in your teaching career: the majority being genuinely supportive people who want to help you succeed in teaching their child. A minority of parents, unfortunately, will be less helpful and some may even prove very difficult to deal with. You should remember at all times that, as discussed previously in this chapter, the parents are the clients and you are the one providing a service: always stay calm and polite when you are speaking to parents, no matter how much they antagonize you. A good way to avoid confrontation is to use some of the tactics you would employ with a difficult student.

I would like to offer you a few brief ideas about how to deal with some different types of parents, although obviously each parent (and each child) is an individual. Again, the way you deal with parents will vary a great deal according to the situation you find yourself in and also the policies of your school or department. The best advice is to concentrate on doing your job as well as you can, and not to worry too much if you do have the occasional conflict.

Supportive parents

Supportive parents are a delight to work with: they believe that you know your job, but they are there to back you up should you ever need it. They encourage their children to do the best they can and to take the work (and homework) you set seriously. If possible, try to involve this type of parent as much as you can with the school, for instance, asking them to visit your class to give a talk or to help individual students with their work.

Over-ambitious parents

It is very difficult to deal with this type of parent. They want the best for their children, but unfortunately their ambitions sometimes outstrip what the children are capable of, or what the students want for themselves. These parents can make life difficult for the teacher as well, asking why you have set particular work and suggesting that you don't know how to do your job. The best policy with this type of parent is probably to humour them as much as possible, but not to alter what you have decided to teach because of them.

Over-protective parents

Some parents worry a great deal about how their children are settling into the school, and because of this probably have a rather negative impact. You should try to answer their worries, particularly if you are the child's tutor, but keep reassuring them that you will look out for their child and contact them if there are any serious problems. The over-protective parent might be a useful candidate for coming into the classroom to help you out. That way, he or she can see the child coping well, and can help with some of the children who need additional assistance.

Parents who abdicate responsibility

This type of parent believes that the child is the school's problem, and that you should deal with any difficulties that come up. They believe that their responsibility ends when the child leaves the home. Again, it is hard to deal with this type of parent, but bear in mind that the child may well see school in a rather negative way and will probably need lots of praise and encouragement.

Potentially abusive parents

If you suspect that a child is being abused at home, either physically or psychologically, you should notify your child protection officer and the appropriate pastoral manager or deputy head at once. They may be aware of the situation, but you would not be doing your job (and you would be failing the child) if you did not make your concerns known. It is not your responsibility to deal with such serious problems and you do not have the specialist knowledge required to do so. Pass your concerns on, in writing, immediately.

DEALING WITH COMPLAINTS

From time to time, parents will complain, either about what you are teaching or about how you are teaching. You will know whether these complaints are justified, and for the most part they will not be, but unfortunately they really are just part of the job. Stick to your guns – if the work you have set is in line with departmental and school policies, if the sanctions you have given are fair and the student has earned them, then you are acting professionally as a teacher. Be confident in yourself: even though you have only just started teaching, you are a professional and have undertaken the appropriate training for your job.

If a parent complains directly to you, perhaps over the telephone or by letter, you should talk to a more experienced member of staff before responding. Your induction tutor, pastoral manager or head of department will have experience in dealing with parents and can help you decide what to do. Explain the situation as clearly as you can, stating exactly what you have done and why. Your colleagues should be more than willing to back you up. If the parent complains indirectly, perhaps to your head of department, find out exactly what they said and again make your position clear. Do not worry too much. As I have said, these complaints really are unavoidable, even for the best and most experienced teachers in a school.

Part V

Just Part of the Job

Chapter 11

Meetings and extra-curricular activities

After a long day at school, you will find at least some of your evenings taken up with meetings and probably with extra-curricular activities as well. Depending on how well they are run, meetings can feel like a very valuable part of your job, or a complete waste of time. The extra-curricular work you do after school will generally offer a much more positive experience. Many of the staff who run these activities do so not because they are required to, but because they genuinely enjoy the experience. In this chapter you can find some ideas about meetings, as well as about the plus and minus sides of extra-curricular work.

THE STAFF MEETING

Generally speaking, there are two kinds of staff meeting: the regular briefing-type meeting which is fairly short and deals with the day-to-day practicalities of running a school, and the formalized meeting of all the staff that will take place approximately once a term. The main features of each type of meeting differ quite substantially.

The staff briefing

Depending on the school you are teaching at, there may be a staff briefing once a day, once or twice a week, or perhaps on a less regular basis. This type of meeting allows the different staff within the school to communicate important information quickly and easily to each other. In a large school this is a useful way of informing all the staff at once of an upcoming event or a particular problem with a student.

This type of meeting will usually be far less formal than the staff meeting and there will probably not be an agenda. The briefing may be opened by the the head or deputy head(s) giving information to the staff, for instance, about promotions or expulsions. The other members of staff may then be invited to raise any points they wish to make.

There are certain members of staff who will normally need to speak at this briefing: special needs staff may give bulletins about the latest student assessments or new IEPs; pastoral managers might give updates on particular students, for instance, if someone in their year or house group has been suspended; heads of department or curriculum co-ordinators may give information about trips or forthcoming events such as training courses in their subject area, and so on. If you have anything you need the entire staff to know urgently, this is the forum at which to do it; it can, however, be very nerve-racking to talk to a staff room full of people.

The formal staff meeting

Formal staff meetings are part of your directed time – the statutory hours that a teacher must work – as opposed to the actual (voluntary) hours you might put in. These formal staff meetings are usually timetabled well in advance on the school calendar. They will normally take place after school (probably in the staff room or another room big enough to take all the staff) or perhaps on an INSET day at the start of term. Formal staff meetings may go on for up to two hours or more. In most cases, though, they would be about an hour long. The head will probably publish an agenda the week before the meeting takes place and put it in your pigeon-hole or on a staff noticeboard.

Often the head and deputy head(s) do most of the speaking at these meetings and they will cover whole-school issues, such as development plans or inspection visits. Depending on the size of your school, you may be required to contribute, or merely to soak up the information that is being given. These meetings may also be given over to group work where you are required to discuss an issue in a smaller group and then report your ideas back to the whole staff.

THE DEPARTMENT/SUBJECT MEETING

In the secondary school you will also have regular department meetings (perhaps once a fortnight/month), at which you discuss subject-specific issues. These may take place before or after school, or perhaps in a lunch-time or free period when everyone in the department is available. In a large department, these meetings are an important means of communicating information between different teachers. If run well, departmental meetings are a valuable source of updating and will also give you the chance to mix more regularly with the other members of your department.

At these meetings, members of the department share information: details of syllabus requirements, upcoming exams, schemes of work, visits, and so on. If someone in your department attends a working party at the school, for instance, on whole-school assessment policies, they might have information to disseminate. Your head of department could also decide to use some of your meeting time to moderate work, for instance, GCSE coursework, or plan termly or yearly schemes.

In the primary school, you may be required to attend meetings devoted to specific curriculum subjects. For instance, the school's literacy co-ordinator might run a meeting about new developments in the literacy strategy. These meetings will offer a good opportunity to pick up new teaching ideas and techniques to use in your own classroom.

THE MEETINGS TRAP

As well as these 'statutory' meetings, there will be many other meetings going on after school. Your presence will not be required at most of these, as attendance is often limited to staff in positions of responsibility. However, there could also be other working parties that meet perhaps once per half-term.

At the start of the year, each department or key stage may be asked to put forward staff to sit on these working parties. Depending on the way your school is set up and run, these meetings are either a complete waste of time, or a very valuable chance to contribute to what happens in the school. As with extra-curricular activities, it can be valuable to be able to say you were on a working party when you apply for other jobs, as it shows you are willing to get involved in every aspect of the way your school is run. Similarly, you may value the chance to meet staff from other departments or areas of the school, and you may have some excellent ideas (or a specialism) of your own that you would like to develop.

Do not feel pressurized into joining these working parties unless you are sure you have the time. No one will mind if an inexperienced teacher does not volunteer to help out, but you could find that others take advantage of you because you are fresh, uncynical and enthusiastic to offer your services. If you can guarantee that you will only have to attend a couple of meetings a term, and do no other work, then it may be worth your while volunteering. However, beware of the 'meetings trap' whereby you end up doing lots of additional paperwork, writing plans, disseminating information to your department, and so on. If you are involved with a lot of extra-curricular activities, for instance, if you teach sport, drama or music, you will have a very good 'get-out clause'.

EXTRA-CURRICULAR ACTIVITIES

People often associate extra-curricular activities with teachers who are specialists in particular subjects, for instance, drama teachers (the school play), music teachers (the school choir and orchestra) and PE teachers (football, netball teams, and so on). However, there is no real reason why this should be so and it is still worth becoming involved with this aspect of the school if you possibly can, even if you do not see yourself as a specialist. Below you can find some thoughts about the different advantages and disadvantages of getting involved with extra-curricular activities.

The advantages

In my experience, the advantages of taking part in extra-curricular activities far outweigh the disadvantages. In some schools (or if you are a teacher of certain subjects) there may be an element of compulsion for you to participate. Even if this is not the case, it is well worth getting involved if you can. Do be careful, though, as an NQT not to take on too much. Here are some thoughts about the advantages of extra-curricular work:

- *Getting to know the students*: Foremost among the advantages of taking part in extra-curricular activities is the opportunity to get to know the students in a more relaxed environment. You will also meet students who are not in your classes, ones you would not normally teach or talk to. Unless you teach in a very small school, it is probable that you will only encounter a fraction of the school population at any one time. When you do meet these children as a teacher, perhaps a year or two later, they will already have had good experiences with you and are likely to feel much more positive about you.

- *Showing yourself as a 'real' person*: Because extra-curricular activities take place outside the constraints of the normal school environment, it is possible to approach them in a more relaxed and natural manner than that which you might use in your classroom. Consequently, the children will get to see an entirely different side of you and this can have considerable benefits in your relationship when they encounter you during the school day.

- *Helping out your colleagues*: Those teachers who do undertake extra-curricular work as part of their job (for instance, drama or PE teachers) will be very grateful for any help you can offer. The nature of teachers means that they will probably find some way to reciprocate in the future.

- *Seeing another side of your students*: It may also surprise you to discover that students considered difficult in academic subjects become completely different during extra-curricular activities. Many of them will have talents in areas you had never suspected and it is always rewarding for both student and teacher to see success and achievement taking place.

- *Useful for the CV*: Being able to show a willingness to participate in all aspects of school life is seen as an indicator of a keen and enthusiastic teacher. It will provide you with a very positive point for your curriculum vitae (CV) and your letters of application for jobs in the future.

- *New skills and experiences*: If you participate in life outside the school day, you will also undergo a wider variety of experiences and develop a range of different skills. For instance, if you do the lighting for your school play, you will extend (or discover) technical skills that could enhance your teaching. You will also show the ability to work as a member of a team, an ability not normally particularly strongly developed in teachers, whose job by its very nature is a solo activity.
- *Personal satisfaction*: Finally, you will find personal satisfaction from taking part in extra-curricular activities. You can stretch and extend yourself, perhaps into areas that you were previously unsure about or in which you lacked confidence.

The disadvantages

There are, of course, some negative aspects to getting involved with activities after school. In my opinion, these are far outweighed by the more positive aspects. However, as an NQT it is important to think carefully before becoming involved, and to balance up the pros and cons. Here are some thoughts about why you might want to limit your involvement:

- *The time commitment*: The most important point to take into account is the time consideration: how much time can you afford to take away from your planning, marking and administrative loads? If, for instance, you get involved with a school football team, you could find yourself working late after school perhaps two or three nights a week. You may also want to accompany your team to matches and these may take place on a Saturday or Sunday morning. A commitment to extra-curricular activities means giving up your own free time.
- *An escalating commitment?*: Once you start getting involved after school, extra-curricular activities have a tendency to escalate. The other staff and the school management see that you are willing, and perhaps try to push you into becoming over-involved and taking on more responsibility than you should.
- *The views of your managers*: On the other hand, the management at your school may feel that inexperienced teachers should be concentrating on developing their classroom practice, and may actively discourage you from involvement. If this is the case for

you, for instance, you might have an induction tutor who feels you should focus on your teaching work, then consider waiting until you have passed your NQT year.

SOME TIPS ON TRIPS

In my experience, one of the most memorable school experiences for many children is the chance to go on a trip. For some, this opportunity may never otherwise come their way, perhaps because of money considerations. Trips can seem like a great adventure for students in which they get out of school and see a little of the real world. Of course, trips also have a very valid educational justification behind them. For the teacher, too, a trip is the chance to get out of school for a day (or more) and get to know the students better in a different environment. So, if you are approached to take part in a trip, for instance, a visit to a museum, an art gallery or the theatre, say 'Yes' immediately. There is no reason why a relatively inexperienced teacher should not organize a trip. If you are interested in doing this, or in taking part in a trip that someone else has arranged, do read the following tips very carefully:

- *Follow the school policy carefully*: First and foremost, I would caution you to ensure that your school or LEA trips policy is followed to the letter. If you are arranging a trip as an NQT, find a more experienced colleague who is willing to support and assist you. There are legal obligations involved with taking students out of school and it is very important that you are aware of these. You are *in loco parentis* – in the role of a parent – and if there are any problems you are legally responsible. You will also need to complete paperwork such as risk assessments and so on. However, as long as you are careful and follow the 'school rules' to the letter, you will find organizing a trip a very worthwhile experience.
- *Have plenty of supervision*: The normal requirement for a staff to student ratio would be around one adult for every ten students, although this varies according to the age of the children. If you are taking a large group, try to find a real range of teachers from different subject areas to accompany them. This will give the children the benefit of a wider range of personalities and will also allow you to get to know some more of the school staff in a more relaxed environment.

- *Be aware of all the administrative jobs*: Before you go you will need to send letters home, asking for permission, and also for a voluntary contribution towards the costs. You will have to collect return slips and money, which can prove to be an administrative nightmare, so make sure you leave sufficient time before the trip to do this. Many schools have a budget set aside to help students who cannot afford the cost of trips and you should check how this works before you start. You should also find out where and how to pay in the money you receive. In reality, you may well find that you have to use your own money (or credit card) in order initially to finance the trip. This fact, along with all the organizational difficulties, is what puts many teachers off organizing and making trips.
- *Organize transport carefully*: If the trip is by coach, you will need to find a suitable company. Ask other staff for advice – geography teachers will often have this information because they have to organize field trips. If the trip is taking place outside of normal school hours, you should arrange a meeting place for your students. At the end of the trip this could be where you will 'drop them off', although you should remain with them until they have all been collected.
- *Keep an eye on behaviour*: The students may become very excited during the trip; it is your duty to calm them down and ensure that they behave themselves. Normally, however, this is not a problem, as they will be enjoying their day out and will not want to jeopardize it with poor behaviour.
- *Put it on your CV*: Finally, bear in mind that organizing trips is also an excellent experience to have on your CV when you apply for jobs. It shows initiative, and also (as with any extra-curricular activity) a willingness to really become involved with your school. If you do not have the opportunity (or confidence) to organize your own trip, try to get invited on one of the trips organized by other members of staff. The advantages of doing so are the same as with extra-curricular activities; and sometimes a day out of school can be just what you need.

Chapter 12

Induction, appraisal and inspection

Your teaching practices will have given you a good idea of what life as a teacher is really like, but it is only during your first year in the profession that you actually *become* a teacher. Part of the whole process of becoming a qualified teacher is passing your NQT year. The actual arrangements for induction or probation vary in different areas of the country, but overall the process has a number of similarities. In this chapter you can find out all about what to expect during your NQT year, including tips on how to do your best during appraisal. In addition, you'll find some advice and ideas about inspection.

Do try not to focus too much on 'passing induction/inspection' or on 'passing your NQT year'. The key to success is to concentrate on what really matters, i.e. how well the children are doing and how you are developing your skills in the classroom to facilitate their learning.

INDUCTION: WHAT TO EXPECT

The government publishes guidelines which specify what should happen during your induction year. Of course, how well these are followed will vary from school to school. If you are lucky, your induction tutor (or mentor) will be experienced, effective and (perhaps most importantly) available when you need to speak to him or her. However, it is also possible that you will have less support from and access to your induction tutor, especially if the person assigned is a more senior manager. It can be difficult as an

NQT to complain if the induction guidelines are not being followed, but do make sure you know exactly what you are entitled to. Remember that it is you who will pass or fail, and this could depend on how well your school supports you. During induction you can expect to receive the following:

- Help and support from experienced teachers.
- Non-contact time to help you cope with and adapt to the workload. (Note: you should not have to teach for more than 90 per cent of a normal timetable.)
- Observations of your lessons.
- Assessments of your teaching, both formal and informal.
- Setting of targets and objectives on which you can work.
- Professional development, for instance, additional training.

For lots more detailed information about exactly what induction involves, see my book *The Guerilla Guide to Teaching* (London: Continuum).

THE ROLE OF THE INDUCTION TUTOR

Your induction tutor will play a vital role when you start teaching: he or she is the person you turn to if you have any questions or problems and will also be responsible for watching some of your lessons to evaluate your progress. The induction tutor should also ensure that you are not taking on too much on top of your lesson preparation and marking. If you are lucky enough to have a good and supportive tutor, this will make your life much easier.

You should aim to have regular meetings with your tutor, in which they set you targets and help you assess your own progress, dealing with any worries that you may have. A little way into your first term, you should discuss your first formal evaluation. Hopefully, your tutor will allow you to choose a particular subject or class for this observation. It is not necessarily beneficial to choose an 'easy' lesson: it may be better to prove to them (and to yourself) that you can deal with more difficult or challenging subjects or students.

GETTING THE MOST FROM YOUR INDUCTION TUTOR

As a new teacher, you may feel at a disadvantage in the relationship between you and your tutor, who will have more (perhaps much more) experience than you. Do bear in mind, though, that your tutor will probably have volunteered for the role and will be keen for you to do well. The tips below will help you in getting the most from your induction tutor, and in developing a good relationship:

- *Be proactive*: As an NQT who is new to the school and the staff, it can be hard to push your own wishes to the fore. Teachers are all very busy people, and it may prove difficult to find as much time as you would like to spend with your induction tutor. However, if you do find that your relationship with your tutor is not developing as you feel it should, then be proactive about the situation rather than sitting back and letting things deteriorate.
- *Set a specific time to meet*: Find out when your tutor is available to sit and talk to you, rather than trying to catch them during a break. It is a good idea to set a specific time (if possible each week) when you can meet for a discussion.
- *Explain your responsibilities*: Let the tutor know what other responsibilities you have taken on, both to show how willing you are, and also to show what your workload is like. The induction tutor should be able to advise you about whether these extra activities are a good idea.
- *Get lots of information*: Ask your tutor early on about what the induction process involves: how many meetings and lesson evaluations you should expect, how much detail you will need to include in your lesson planning and longer-term schemes of work.
- *Be honest about any difficulties*: If you are having problems, don't keep them to yourself. Share your worries with your induction tutor and he or she should be able to help and advise you. When it comes to a lesson evaluation, if the class is a difficult one, be honest with your tutor and explain any problems you have had. It will prove impressive for the tutor to see you trying (and succeeding) with a difficult class or lesson. Having said this, do not get your tutor to watch the proverbial 'nightmare' class or lesson, at least in the first term.

PREPARING FOR APPRAISAL

Even experienced teachers are required to undergo regular appraisal or evaluation, and this type of 'testing' should be seen as an important and useful part of your job. Appraisers take different approaches when they evaluate a class: some like to get involved, moving around to question the students, to look at their books (and check your marking) and to help anyone who needs it; others may simply sit in a corner at the back of the room and watch what goes on from there. You could, of course, ask your appraiser if they will assist you in a particular part of your lesson. This would demonstrate initiative on your part and, if your appraiser happens to be a teacher in your subject area, he or she could be a valuable resource for you.

When you (or your appraiser) have chosen a lesson for evaluation, you should prepare carefully for this formalized review. Generally speaking, this is a very worthwhile process and one that you should get used to. It is almost certain that, at some point in your teaching career, you will have to face an official inspection. You will, of course, have faced appraisal by your tutors many times during your training at college. Indeed, recent graduates are perhaps better prepared for this process than those who have been in teaching for a long time.

There are some things that you should do to ensure that you stand the best chance of receiving a good report. Many of the tips given in Part Two of this book will come in handy when you are being appraised. You might find it useful to reread the sections on preparing for your first lessons and controlling your classes, particularly the 'Ten tried and tested tips' on pp. 38–45. You will have many things on your mind when you are being appraised, but it is important for you to show just how good a classroom teacher you really are. The tips below will help you do just this:

- *Show your appraiser the lesson plan*: Your tutor will probably ask to see a copy of your lesson plan beforehand but, if this does not happen, you can demonstrate how organized you are by doing so. The tutor may also be able to give you advice, for instance, if he or she feels that you will not be showing a sufficiently wide range of skills to be evaluated, or if you are aiming to do too much in the lesson time available.
- *Use a mixture of approaches*: Your appraiser wants to see that you are utilizing a variety of methods in your teaching: for instance, the teacher giving instructions, the students taking part in discussions, doing individual work, and so on. More ideas

about this are given in Chapter 2 in 'Balanced lesson planning' on pp. 19–24. He or she also wants to see the students engaged in a variety of activities, although you should avoid the temptation to have too many different things going on at once as this could create discipline problems.

- *Be well prepared*: If you are planning to use any equipment, for instance, a video clip to illustrate a subject you are covering, do ensure well beforehand that it is available and working. If you are going to need materials such as paper, pens, paints or photocopies, there is nothing worse than having to scrabble around five minutes before the lesson trying to sort them out. Similarly, if you are planning a practical demonstration, it is probably worth going through it once beforehand to ensure that you know exactly what you are doing.
- *Use interesting resources*: Lots of ideas about finding interesting resources are given in Chapter 4. It is always worth being inventive with the resources you use, as the students will respond more positively and your appraiser will hopefully be impressed and interested in your ideas.
- *Stick to what you know*: Now is not the time to try something completely new with your class – you will confuse the students and you may well 'throw' them into misbehaviour. They will be aware that something different is going on, and may comment on it, which could be rather embarrassing for you.
- *Take care with timing*: Your appraiser will watch the opening and ending of your lesson particularly closely, as one of the most obvious signs of a well prepared and organized teacher is how they manage these times. Make sure you have an orderly start and finish. Remember that you may get caught up in your teaching and not notice that time is running out, so keep a close eye on the clock.
- *Demonstrate your classroom management skills*: You should aim to impress your appraiser not only by good subject content, but also by how well you can control the students. In the run-up to your evaluation, refer the class back to the boundaries you set at the beginning of term, particularly if it has been a while since you last discussed them.
- *Remain positive*: It is very tempting, when you are under the stress of being 'tested', to react negatively to any children who do play up. Stick closely to the boundaries you have set and give out

sanctions (and rewards) firmly and fairly, just as you have been doing. If you look as if you mean business, and if they have built up respect for you, the class will work with you and for you.

- *Warn the class?*: This is a matter of individual taste: should you warn the class that someone will be watching them, or just wait and see how they react when your appraiser turns up? If you do warn them in advance, just say something like: '*Mrs Johnson will be coming to watch our class on Thursday to see what we're doing and how we're getting on.*' Do not tell them directly that it is you who are being appraised, although some of them will probably work it out for themselves.
- *Marking*: Do ensure that your marking is fully up to date. However, do not alter your marking policy just because your appraiser is going to be looking at the books. The students will soon pipe up: '*Miss, you never normally mark our books like this!*'
- *Relax*: Above all, remember you are only just starting out as a teacher – you don't have to be perfect yet. No one will realistically expect you to have mastered every aspect of being a teacher, otherwise there would be no point in appraisal. Even the most experienced teachers can have an 'off' day. Remember that your appraiser is a teacher too – they will understand!

FEEDBACK

After the appraisal, make sure you get the feedback you are entitled to, as soon as possible. Teachers are busy people, but there is no point in being appraised if you do not find out what you did right or wrong and why. For your formal assessments, you should receive both verbal feedback and a formalized written evaluation, which may take a little time to prepare. Once you have heard what your appraiser has to say, discuss your own opinions with them. They will want to see that you can evaluate your own teaching. In fact, one of the best ways for you to improve and progress is by learning to see what went wrong or right in your own lessons, and why.

Your appraiser should also set you some targets and objectives to work towards for your next evaluation. There might be about three of these, and they should cover the problem areas that the induction tutor feels you need to work on. You should receive a copy of your formal written evaluation and the school will put another copy on your personnel file. Your appraiser will probably ask you to read the evaluation and to sign it to show that you have had the opportunity to discuss it.

SURVIVING INSPECTION

So, how unlucky do you have to be for your school to receive an inspection when you have only just started teaching? Statistically, the chances must be quite slim, but it is by no means an impossibility. The longer you stay at any school, the more chance there is that the inspectors will pay a visit sooner or later. The 'failing' schools and 'failing' teachers that the inspectors root out receive a great deal of publicity, but, on the other hand, all the successful and thriving schools seem to get very little.

Preparing for inspection

Even if you are at a school which you believe is going to do badly in its inspection, remember that as an inexperienced teacher you will have very little responsibility. As long as you are doing your job to the best of your ability, and consistently striving to improve your teaching, there is very little for you to worry about. If you came into teaching straight from college, all the latest developments in the profession will be fresh in your memory. You may also be more enthusiastic and have more energy than the teachers who have been in the profession for a longer time.

Your school will receive warning that it is going to receive an inspection well in advance. Indeed, they will probably know (and tell you) at your interview if an inspection is coming up. This advance warning has its good and bad points. It gives the school plenty of time to prepare, to get documentation in place, to help the weaker teachers improve (and perhaps exclude some of the more difficult students). However, it also leads to a climate of expectation in which rumours abound about the horrors of inspection.

The myths

As the arrival of the inspectors gets closer and closer, the myths will start to multiply and take on a life of their own. The senior managers at your school will, of course, be under a lot of stress at this time. They may warn you that everything you say will be taken down and used in evidence against the school; that the inspectors will be particularly concerned with your subject or age range; that every lesson plan and department handbook will be closely scrutinized.

It is possible that you will have to use a particular format to prepare your lesson plans and your department may work itself into a frenzy, getting handbooks and schemes of work in place for the inspection (handbooks and schemes of work that will never see the light of day again after the inspectors have gone). You will be warned that, if the inspectors come to see you and don't like what they see, they will keep returning again and again to your classes. The myth will probably circulate that you are sacked on the spot if you 'fail' (i.e. if you receive a bad score for a particular lesson).

The reality

In reality, it is likely that observations of your lessons will happen no more than a few times in the week of inspection. In many schools there are relatively few inspectors to go around and some inspectors will cover more than one subject or age range. In an inspection at my previous school, when we reached Thursday of the inspection week and I still had not been 'seen', my head of department had to *request* that someone observes one of my lessons so that the inspectors could see the practice going on in our department. This situation may, of course, vary in a smaller school or at primary level. However, even if you are 'seen' by the inspectors on several occasions, this does not mean that they have found anything wrong with your teaching.

When an inspector arrives in your lesson they will probably ask for a copy of the lesson plan and you should have this easily to hand. If they do not ask for your lesson plan, hand it over anyway. After all, you have spent all that time preparing for your moment of glory and you should show the inspectors exactly what you are capable of. Irritatingly, this means that you will have to have detailed plans ready for every lesson that you are due to teach that week. However, the amount of information required is not great. It is fairly unlikely that the inspector, with a full timetable of classes to watch, will be able to stay for the entire length of the lesson. It is of course likely that they will leave just as the best bit of your lesson begins!

Inspection and the NQT

As a new teacher you will probably have no curriculum responsibility and will only be responsible for ensuring that you teach your own class or classes properly. This means that if a secondary school department is disorganized, it will not be you that comes under fire. The head of your department has full responsibility for ensuring that all documentation is correct and in place: schemes of work, handbooks, and so on. If an inspector does come to watch your lessons, they will know that you are an inexperienced teacher and they should take this fact into account.

Part VI

Onwards and Upwards

Chapter 13

Professional development and promotion

Towards the end of your first year in the profession, you may find yourself considering your future. You will be encouraged to consider how you might develop yourself as a professional, whether this is by applying for promotion or by taking courses to learn new skills and further your teaching qualifications. In this chapter I deal with the issues of professional development and promotion. Even if you decide not to step onto the promotions ladder at this stage, it is still worth considering when and how you might wish to move onwards and upwards within your current school, or elsewhere.

INSET

Your training as a teacher does not end once you qualify and it is likely, particularly if your school has access to a good training budget, that you will get the chance to go on INSET, or in-service training, courses. I would advise that you take every opportunity that is offered to you to go on courses. There are a number of reasons why you should do this:

- *Professional development*: Courses offer you a chance to develop and update your knowledge about teaching, whether this is about a specific subject, or an area such as behaviour management.
- *A chance for a break*: In addition to this, you will also have a day, or days, out of school. This can be especially useful in the second

term, when you could do with a break from the day to day routine of school.

- *Useful for your CV*: It is also important for your CV that you can show an interest in maintaining your subject knowledge and extending your skills. Going on a course gives you the chance to refresh yourself, both personally and professionally, and to demonstrate your enthusiasm to continue learning after you have qualified.

If you are academically minded, if you are seeking promotion to the highest level, or if you would like to move into further education, it is useful to do a post-graduate qualification, such as an MA. It is sometimes possible to do this part-time with the assistance of your school (both financially and with your timetable). Unfortunately, this situation is becoming rarer as schools and local authorities are forced to make budget cuts and savings. You may also find that you do not have the time or energy to go to evening classes when you first start teaching.

AIMING FOR PROMOTION?

At some point in your teaching career, you will need to decide just how far you would like to advance. Towards the end of your NQT year is a good time to do this – you will still (hopefully) be enthusiastic towards the profession, and you will have the benefit of a year's experience of what the job is really like. Below are some thoughts about aiming for promotion for you to consider:

- *Promotions rely on many different factors*: In my experience, promotions in teaching rely on a number of issues, not just how good you are at your job. Being in the right place at the right time when a post becomes available is often an important element in gaining promotion.
- *You may need to move school to find promotion*: Because of the limited movement available within any one school, both in terms of the jobs available and also the fact that teachers have a tendency to stay where they are, you may simply find that no promotion opportunities occur. In this case you will have to think carefully about whether you want or need to move to another school to find promotion.
- *The nature of your job will change*: As you get promoted, your

actual teaching timetable will generally become a little lighter. For instance, a head of department in a secondary school may only teach 18 hours a week, while the 'normal' teacher has 21 hours. A head of year may only have a timetable of 15 hours a week to allow them time to do their job effectively: meeting parents, attending case conferences, and so on. You need to decide at a fairly early stage whether you want to spend less and less time in the classroom. If your eventual aim is to become a deputy head or head of a school, be aware that you will find yourself spending very little time actually teaching, and far more on management and administrative tasks.

- *There's nothing wrong with staying in the classroom*: There is quite a lot of pressure in teaching to aim for promotion, but do bear in mind that there is no compulsion to do so. Some teachers dedicate their careers to becoming the best teacher that they can: they do not want to leave the classroom or take on any management responsibilities, they find more satisfaction in committing themselves to their students. The new threshold and advanced skills teacher arrangements are now recognizing the value of classroom expertise.

- *Promotion means better pay*: Of course, one of the reasons many teachers aim for promotion is financial: as a classroom teacher you will reach the ceiling of the standard pay scale after around seven years. The points that come with promotion will boost your salary, although never by a substantial amount. Even the head of a large secondary school will only be earning a fraction of what he or she could get in a commensurate position in industry.

- *Different types of promotion are available*: If you do decide to aim for promotion, there are generally two types of promoted position: pastoral and curriculum. A pastoral role involves looking after the students' needs and welfare in the school as a whole, while a curriculum role includes teaching and managing a specific subject (or a group of subjects in a faculty).

TYPES OF PROMOTION

Table 13.1 demonstrates the most likely route for promotion in a secondary school and the points that could be given for each job (although these are subject to a lot of variation). Clearly there are

Table 13.1 *Promotion in a secondary school*

Pastoral	Curriculum
Deputy head of year/house – 1 point	Key Stage 3/4 co-ordinator – 2 points – often only English, maths and science.
Head of year/house – 2-4 points	Deputy head of department – 2-3 points
Deputy head – depends on the size and type of school (also assistant headteacher posts now available)	Head of department – 3-5 points – depending on the subject and size of department.
Headteacher – depends on the size and type of school.	Head of faculty – 4-5 points – often a senior teacher.

many pathways to the different posts available, for instance, a head of year may move across to a head of department post if they have sufficient subject experience. In the primary school the options are a little more limited – here you might move into a subject co-ordinator's role before starting to climb the ladder to senior management.

THE ADVANTAGES OF PROMOTION

When you are deciding whether or not to go for promotion, it is well worth taking some time to consider the pros and cons. The advantages of taking a promoted post would include:

- *A salary increase*: As mentioned before, one of the main and most obvious attractions of taking a promotion is the resulting increase in salary you can expect. However, there are clearly other benefits, as the salary increase is not exactly enormous.
- *More responsibility*: As you are promoted, you will have more and more responsibility: responsibility for increasing numbers of students and for managing other members of staff.
- *Increased job satisfaction*: This additional responsibility can lead to increased job satisfaction and you will also have the chance to

make more of an impact on the policies and philosophies that your school uses. Consequently, you will probably feel that you have more of a say in the way things are run, and this can be very satisfying for the teacher who sees the negative results of ineffective management.

- *Developing your subject area*: If you become a head of department or faculty, you can influence and indeed dictate the procedures used within your area. You are also in a position to develop the role of your subject within the school. You will be employing, managing, developing and promoting other teachers within your area and this can be very rewarding. You will have your own budget to manage for buying books, resources, and so on.
- *'Better' relationships with the students*: As you go up the scale of status within any school, you will receive a degree of instant respect from the students. This is obviously qualified by how they see you as a teacher, but students are clearly going to give more (or more instant) respect to their head of year than to a 'normal' teacher. Behaviour in your classes may therefore improve as a result of promotion, although this is by no means automatic.

THE DISADVANTAGES OF PROMOTION

Just as there are a number of positive sides to taking promotion, so you will also need to weigh up the more negative aspects of a change in role before going for a more senior post. These disadvantages would include:

- *A changing, more stressful role*: In a promoted post you will have to play more and more of a managerial role in your school. Despite being trained to work in the classroom, you will have to do a very different job, requiring very different skills. You will have to manage teachers as well as students, both jobs that are very difficult and highly stressful.
- *A changing relationship with your colleagues*: Be aware, too, that being promoted means a change in the way you work with and relate to other teachers. For instance, it can be hard to have to deal with a teacher who is not doing his or her job properly.
- *Working outside your area of expertise*: If you are promoted to a

managerial post, you will have to learn to run a budget, which is not easy if you have no financial experience. In a pastoral role, you will move further and further away from your subject, perhaps one of the main motivating factors for a career in teaching.

- *Working with difficult students*: As a manager you are likely to spend a lot of time dealing with the more difficult students, whose problems (and the problems they create for their teachers) you must try to solve. You will also have to interact with parents or guardians, again often the parents of the problem students. One of the joys of teaching is interaction with bright, well motivated students, and this will lessen as you move up the scale in favour of disciplining those who have done something wrong.
- *A changing persona*: Taking on a role with more status will also require you to adopt a different persona to that of the classroom teacher. A 'normal' teacher can, after a few years' experience, get away with a more relaxed style with their students. This is not really an option if you are a pastoral manager or deputy head. You will have to be 'in role' at all times, dressing and behaving appropriately. As a head of year or house you will probably have to run assemblies for a large group of students and this can be a rather frightening prospect.
- *Additional workload and responsibility*: As you advance up the scale of responsibility you will have to attend a wide range of after-school meetings and this will take up much of your free time at the end of each day. The increased administrative workload that comes with promotion may mean that you also have to sacrifice involvement in extra-curricular activities And of course, the higher up the scale you go, the more likely it is that 'the buck stops with you' if anything does go wrong.

Chapter 14

Moving on

Some teachers choose to stay at the same school for a number of years, while others find themselves keen to move on quickly (perhaps because of a negative experience). If you are considering moving on at the end of your NQT year, this is a decision that you should spend a good deal of time thinking about. It may be that you need to make a fresh start in a new school, or even that you are considering actually leaving the profession. The information and ideas in this chapter will help you decide whether now, or later, is the time to change jobs.

THE RIGHT SCHOOL?

After your first year, you should have a fair idea about whether the school that you are working in is the right school for you. However, it is important to differentiate between the inevitable tiredness associated with the end of the year and the need to find a new school (or career). There is absolutely no point in going through the work associated with looking for another teaching job (you remember – the endless form filling and letters of application) if you are going to be moving from the proverbial frying pan into the fire.

You could look around your local area to see if there are any schools that interest you, and perhaps ask to make visits to some of them, particularly if there are jobs available. Remember, there is a lot more to choosing a school than just the quality of its students.

Remember also that no school is perfect: what you need to decide is whether the good points about your school outweigh the bad. Moving after only one or two years at a school is a big decision to make – especially as you will just be becoming familiar with the way things work.

Think also about how long you want to stay in one place: I believe that one of the biggest problems with the teaching profession is the temptation to stay at the same school for a long time – after a while, it simply becomes easier not to move. You know the children, the staff, the systems, you may have gained promotion within your department or subject area, but is it necessarily beneficial for you or for the school to stay for those reasons? In order to help you decide whether you need to move or not, think about how your school scores in each of the following areas.

Management

Are the managers (head, deputy head(s), heads of department, pastoral managers) at your school approachable and willing to support and develop their teachers or have they lost touch with what it means to be in a classroom? Do the senior staff of the school spend time in the classroom, or simply sit in an office, handing down commands from above? How have the managers supported you during your NQT year, and have they resolved any problems that you have experienced?

Staff

Do the staff at your school relate well to each other and support each other's ideas and work or have they become cynical and lazy, either through disillusionment with the job or with the school? Do they tend to talk about the school in a positive or negative way? Do the different departments within your school work together or in isolation? One of the signs of a good secondary school is a lot of interaction between the various different subject areas.

Another consideration is how well you get on with the staff at your school: you will be spending a lot of time working alongside them – do you respect their professionalism, and do you have at least a few things in common? Do you get on well with the support staff and other people who work at the school, and have a positive working relationship with these vital members of staff?

Support systems

Think about who you can turn to if you have a problem. In theory it should be your line manager, but does this work in reality? A good school should support and develop its new (and existing) staff, so consider how supportive your school has been to you as a new or relatively inexperienced teacher. Would you say that the staff in your school support each other outside their own classrooms? Think about who supports the students in your school when they have problems and whether their problems are dealt with properly or swept under the carpet. Consider also who supports any teachers with problems and how this is done: for instance, does 'staff development' really consist of persuading old (and expensive) staff to leave?

Your department

In secondary schools heads of departments are increasingly asked to become managers, and some of them are just not cut out for this role. Ask yourself how well your head of department suits this role and whether you believe it is important for him or her to fulfil this managerial part of the job. For instance, if some members of the department are not pulling their weight, will your head of department clamp down on them or just ignore the problem? Of course, some heads of department are excellent despite not being managers as such, so consider also whether you are gaining valuable insights and experience from yours. Another consideration is whether you are getting the opportunities you need within your department or school, both in terms of teaching (A level, top sets, a wide range of classes, and so on) and also in terms of promotion.

The students

Do the children at your school show respect for each other, for their teachers and for their environment, and is there a good mix of students who all get along with each other? It can be very wearing to work in a school where there is difficult behaviour, but this is also a challenge that you may miss if you move to that grammar school in Surrey. Think carefully about what you want out of teaching. Single sex schools or 'good' schools may be easier to teach in, but the increased load in marking and preparation can quickly make up for the lack of behaviour problems. Above all, do you find the students interesting and challenging to teach? This is what you must spend most of your day doing, so think long and hard about this one.

The curriculum

Is your school innovative in the way it approaches the curriculum and are the managers up to date with the latest thoughts, ideas and innovations? Think too about the way your school organizes the curriculum: does your subject or age range get as much priority and resources as you would like or as you think it deserves? In a secondary school, how are the subjects divided: are there faculties where several subjects are grouped together, or do the departments remain very much divided?

Administration, paperwork and meetings

Consider whether your school makes every effort to ensure that it keeps these time-consuming aspects of the job to a minimum. When you come to write reports, do you (and other teachers) consider them a vital and informative method of communicating with the students' home, or are they an ineffective use of your time? When you attend meetings, do you find that they are efficiently run, interesting and a valuable part of school life? Are you given a chance to contribute to the decision-making process about the future direction of your school, or is only a token gesture paid towards genuine consultation with all the staff?

Buildings and facilities

The place in which you work will have a significant impact on you, both in terms of how and what you teach, but also in the way that you and the students regard the school itself. If there is a lot of graffiti and the buildings are all very run down with a lack of facilities, it can have a real impact on the way the children behave in the classroom. Think about whether the room or rooms you teach in are adequate for you and, if you have any complaints about your environment, whether they are taken seriously and dealt with quickly or not.

Promotion prospects

If you are looking for promotion, you may need to move schools to find it, depending on what is currently available at your school. Ask yourself whether your managers consider your 'professional development' important and how they are going about promoting this aspect of your work.

Extra-curricular activities

Are there a variety of well supported extra-curricular activities at your school? This is usually, although not always, a sign of a good school as it indicates that both the staff and the students are keen and well motivated. If there are extra-curricular activities, do a variety of staff get involved, or is the job of running them left to just a couple of departments or the more enthusiastic teachers? Are the parents and guardians keen to get involved with the day to day life of the school, perhaps helping out with after-school clubs?

REFERENCES

When you apply for your next job the school will usually ask for two referees, probably your head and your head of department or line manager. If you are efficient and get on well with them, you should have no problem getting good references. Make sure they have a list of all those 'extras' you have been involved with, such as extra-curricular activities and working parties. Do warn your referees that you have applied for a new job *before* they receive a request for references: it is only polite and will improve the chances of your receiving a good reference. Try to make sure that they also have an idea of the type of job you are applying for, so they can adapt their reference to suit it.

APPLYING FOR JOBS

As the year passes, you will take part in many different aspects of school life, so do make sure that you keep a note of all the 'little extras' that you contribute to your school. There is nothing worse than coming to write the letter of application for your next job, only to realise that you cannot remember which working parties you were on, how many plays or concerts you helped with, and so on. Write *everything* down as you go along. Schools want to know that you are an enthusiastic teacher who likes to get involved with all aspects of the life of the school. You should demonstrate in your letter of application how you have done this at your current school.

Even if you are not desperate to move, bear in mind that if you get an interview for a job it will be good experience for you (and will get you a day out of school). Going for an interview will also demonstrate to your managers that you are looking for further development in your career. If you are an asset to the teaching staff at your school, they may decide that they do not want to lose you, and consequently try to offer you some sort of internal promotion or development. Be realistic about the jobs that you apply for – there is not usually much point in applying for a job which is more than two points above yours in terms of salary.

IS TEACHING THE JOB FOR YOU?

After training for a specific qualification, there is a real temptation to remain with teaching, even if you are not sure that it is the right job for you. At the end of your first year you will have gained some experience and can make a more rational judgement about your choice of career. Do bear in mind, however, that teaching becomes easier the more experienced you become – the first year or two is always hard, no matter how talented a teacher you are.

Think very carefully (during your lovely, long summer holidays) if you are having doubts about teaching. Perhaps have a chat with an experienced member of staff who you can trust to be discreet. Remember also that you may just be in the wrong school or teaching the wrong type of students for you (see 'The right school?' in this chapter). The following lists give some of the plus and minus points of teaching as a profession and may be helpful to you in deciding whether teaching is the career for you.

The rewards

- You are your own boss – to a large extent you teach what you want.
- You are working with the subject that you enjoy, day after day.
- There is good job security and pay rises are automatic.
- The job is as creative as you want to make it.
- The job is as big as you want to make it.
- You can make a *real* difference to your children.
- You can form lasting relationships with students and staff.
- If you are good, your children will always remember you.
- There is excellent variety from day to day.
- You can gain valuable experience of a variety of jobs and situations.
- The actual school day is very short.
- It is a good job to combine with having a family.
- The teachers' pension is a good perk.
- The holidays really are very good indeed – this is a *big* perk. (If you're not convinced about this, just ask any office worker who only gets 20 days annual leave!)

The negative aspects

- The job is physically and emotionally tiring.
- The job expands to meet the extent of your dedication.
- You will encounter difficult and even disturbed children (and parents).
- You may be put at risk of injury from these students.
- The nature of the job can lead to cynicism.
- The salary will never be brilliant and only rises very slowly.
- Your friends in other professions will rapidly start earning (a lot) more.
- There is a lack of genuine promotion prospects for many teachers.
- Ironically, experienced teachers become too expensive for some schools.
- You will often have to work late, in your own time, to do a good job.
- You may be too tired to appreciate those lovely long holidays.

LEAVING

So, you have made the decision to go, and now the moment has come. You have told your children and been faced with reactions from '*Great!*' to '*Please, Miss/Sir, don't leave.*' Leaving really is a double-edged sword – on the one hand you will find out how your students really feel about you (hopefully good), on the other hand you will be leaving behind colleagues and children that you genuinely care about, having worked with them very closely for a long time. You may also feel guilty about leaving some secondary level classes half-way through a course. Don't – if you use this as a reason not to leave, you will never get out of your first school.

On your last day you will hopefully receive lots of cards and presents. You may have to give a leaving speech, but do remember one thing before you list all the grievances you have about the school or the head – you may need a reference from him or her in the future!

Finally, I would like to wish you luck in the future, wherever and whatever you teach. As I said at the start of this book, you have made a wonderful choice of career. Try to look on the difficult times as a challenge and enjoy those indescribable moments of joy when you make a new discovery with a class, help a weak student to succeed, or when your children tell you just what you mean to them. It is a rare and very special job that can offer you all this and more.

Appendix

Abbreviations

Like many other professions, teaching has a language all of its own, and one that is changing all the time, as the latest buzz words and new terms come into play. This can prove surprisingly confusing to the teacher just starting out in the profession, especially because of the huge number of acronyms or abbreviations that the teaching profession uses. You might hear a group of colleagues discussing 'ADHD' or 'EBD', but you will need to know what these letters stand for before you can understand what they are saying. This appendix provides a useful reference guide to many abbreviated terms.

A level	Advanced level	**CPD**	Continuing Professional Development
ADD	Attention Deficit Disorder	**CPO**	Child Protection Officer
ADHD	Attention Deficit Hyperactivity Disorder	**DfES**	Department for Education and Skills
AR&R	Assessment, Recording and Reporting	**EAL**	English as an Additional Language
AS level	Advanced Subsidiary level	**EBD**	Emotional/Behavioural Disorder
ATL	Association of Teachers and Lecturers	**EdPsyc**	Educational Psychologist
BEd	Bachelor of Education	**ESL**	English as a Second Language
BT	Beginning Teacher	**EWO**	Education Welfare Officer
CDG	Curriculum Development Group		

GCSE	General Certificate of Secondary Education	**NQT**	Newly Qualified Teacher
GNVQ	General National Vocational Qualification	**NUT**	National Union of Teachers
GRTP	Graduate and Registered Teacher Programmes	**NVQ**	National Vocational Qualification
GTC	General Teaching Council	**OFSTED**	Office for Standards in Education
GTP	Graduate Teacher Programme	**PAT**	Professional Association of Teachers
GTTR	Graduate Teacher Training Registry	**PGCE**	Post-Graduate Certificate in Education
HMCI	Her Majesty's Chief Inspector of Schools	**PSHE**	Personal, Social and Health Education
HMI	Her Majesty's Inspector of Schools	**PTA**	Parent-Teacher Association
HOD	Head of Department	**QTS**	Qualified Teacher Status
HOY	Head of Year	**RTP**	Registered Teacher Programme
ICT	Information and Communications Technology	**SAT**	Statutory Assessment Tasks
IEP	Individual Education Plan	**SCITT**	School Centred Initial Teacher Training
INSET	In-Service Training	**SEN**	Special Educational Needs
ITT	Initial Teacher Training	**SENCO**	Special Educational Needs Co-ordinator
KS	Key Stage	**SLT**	Senior Leadership Team
LEA	Local Education Authority	**SMT**	Senior Management Team
MFL	Modern Foreign Languages	**SpLD**	Specific Learning Difficulty
NASUWT	National Association of Schoolmasters/Union of Women Teachers	**STRB**	School Teachers' Review Body
NLS	National Literacy Strategy	**TES**	The Times Educational Supplement
NNS	National Numeracy Strategy	**TTA**	Teacher Training Agency